Richard A. Swanson
Editor-in-Chief

Action Learning

Successful Strategies for Individual,

Team, and Organizational Development

Lyle Yorks, Judy O'Neil

& Victoria J. Marsick, Editors

THE ACADEMY OF HUMAN RESOURCE DEVELOPMENT

Advances in Developing Human Resources (ISSN 1523-4223) is a quarterly monograph series published by the Academy of Human Resource Development and Berrett-Koehler Communications, Inc.

Academy of Human Resource Development
P.O. Box 25113
Baton Rouge, LA 70894-5113

Berrett-Koehler Communications, Inc.
8 California Street, Suite 610
San Francisco, CA 94111-4825

Copyright © 1999 by the Academy of Human Resource Development. All rights reserved. No part of this publication may be reproduced, distributed, or transmitted in any form or by any means, including photocopying, recording, or other electronic or mechanical methods, without the prior written permission of the publishers, except in the case of brief quotations embodied in critical reviews and certain other noncommercial uses permitted by copyright law. For permission requests, write to Berrett-Koehler Communications, addressed "Attention: Permissions Coordinator," at the address above.

Subscription Orders: Please send subscription orders to Berrett-Koehler Communications, PO Box 565, Williston, VT 05495, or call 800-929-2929, or fax 802-864-7626. Subscriptions cost $79 for individuals and $125 for institutions. All orders must be prepaid in U.S. dollars or charged to Visa, MasterCard, or American Express. For orders outside the United States, please add $15 for surface mail or $30 for air mail.

Librarians are encouraged to write for a free sample issue.

Standing Orders: By designating your subscription as a "Standing Order" that will remain in effect until you cancel it, you will save both yourself and Berrett-Koehler the paperwork of annual renewal notices, and you will receive a 10 percent discount from the annual subscription rate.

Multiple Copies: Ten or more copies of a single issue of *Advances in Developing Human Resources* can be purchased at a 20 percent discount. Please contact Berrett-Koehler Communications sales department, PO Box 565, Williston VT 05495-9900; call 800-929-2929; fax to 802-864-7626; or visit www.bkconnection.com.

Editorial Correspondence: Address editorial correspondence and inquiries to Richard A. Swanson, Editor-in-Chief, *Advances in Developing Human Resources*, University of Minnesota, 1954 Buford Avenue, Suite 425, St. Paul, MN 55108, USA. E-mail: swanson2@cris.com

 Printed in the United States of America on acid-free and recycled paper.
ISBN 1-58376-022-9

Postmaster: Please send address changes to the Berrett-Koehler address above.
Cover Design: Carolyn Deacy Design, San Francisco, CA
Production: Pleasant Run Publishing Services, Williamsburg, VA

Contents

Preface v
Lyle Yorks, Judy O'Neil, and Victoria J. Marsick

1. Action Learning: Theoretical Bases and Varieties of Practice 1
   Lyle Yorks, Judy O'Neil, and Victoria J. Marsick
   Four approaches to action learning and their different outcomes are presented.
2. Issues in the Design and Implementation of an Action Learning Initiative 19
   Judy O'Neil and Robert L. Dilworth
   The authors discuss a practical strategy for planning action learning initiatives for each of the four approaches.
3. Facilitating Action Learning: The Role of the Learning Coach 39
   Judy O'Neil
   How to move from the role of trainer to the role of learning coach is examined.
4. Transfer of Learning from Action Learning Programs to the Organizational Setting 56
   Lyle Yorks, Sharon Lamm, and Judy O'Neil
   The authors analyze what is required for learning to take hold in the workplace.
5. Action Learning for Personal Development and Transformative Learning 75
   Robert L. Dilworth and Verna J. Willis
   Insights into the personal journey of development and renewal that occur through action learning are presented.

6. **Organizational Culture Change Through Action Learning**   83
   Glenn E. Nilson
   Action learning's effect on organizational culture change is discussed.

7. **Lessons for Implementing Action Learning**   96
   Lyle Yorks, Victoria J. Marsick, and Judy O'Neil
   The authors offer sage advice for those wanting to carry out an action learning initiative.

Appendix: Resources for Action Learning   114
Mary B. Ragno

Index   117
The Authors   123

Preface

Lyle Yorks
Judy O' Neil
Victoria J. Marsick

In a multinational food products company, an action learning team's recommendations for change result in savings of over $500,000 in a single division in the company. The company is awarded a Corporate Excellence award by a national human resource management association in the process.

Struggling with breaking down strong business unit boundaries that had existed for years in the organization, a company creates a cross-functional action learning team to put together a plan for globally centralizing its materials management process. The very people in those business units who would be affected by this centralization work together to come to a consensus on a plan that anticipated and addressed the issues driven by existing business unit boundaries created by the change.

An organization in a highly regulated industry has to move rapidly into a competitive environment. There has been resistance from managers and employees to the kind of changes needed to address this challenge. After involvement in an action learning effort, individuals say things such as, "Learning is ongoing; it never ends. I've learned how to learn. We've changed our outlook to 'we' and will go out to meet the competition."

Stories such as these have fostered increasing interest in the use of action learning as an intervention that can produce individual, team, and organizational learning and improve organizational performance. This interest is not without its problems and dilemmas. Action learning is an approach to working with people that uses work on an actual project or problem as a vehicle for learning. Although action learning programs can take different forms, the term *action learning* is often applied to activities that are not in the tradition of action learning. Sometimes learning activities that are far from the tradition of action learning are labeled action learning. Examples of such mislabeling are simulations and outdoor adventure learning activities. This usage creates confusion, leading some people and organizations to assume they are already doing action learning before they understand the concept. Others may erroneously attribute outcomes (either positive or negative) to action learning that are not, in fact, the result of this learning.

Second, within the action learning tradition there are different approaches, and they produce different kinds of learning experiences. These differences are not always readily apparent in the literature, which can be confusing to someone seeking to learn about action learning and make decisions regarding its appropriateness for his or her own organization.

Third, as more organizations engage in action learning, there is a danger that action learning will become the latest "flavor of the month." Poorly positioned action learning programs can encounter strong resistance from participants as the process takes them out of their comfort zone and confronts them with considerable ambiguity.

Overview of the Book

This book provides a framework for understanding the variations of action learning practice, lays out the implications of different approaches for program design and facilitation, discusses how learning is facilitated in action learning, and demonstrates the kind of learning that takes place at the individual, team, and organizational levels. Drawing on their recent research and experience, chapter authors emphasize implications for practice.

As an area of human resource development practice, action learning rests on sound adult learning theory. Despite its relatively recent popularity in the training and development literature, it enjoys a long tradition of success built on effective practice. This book extends that tradition. Although the principles of action learning allow it to be applied very flexibly, there are certain foundational concepts that provide the basis for its practice.

We first examine theory and practices that help organize the existing literature in a way that we have found very helpful for those seeking to understand which approach to action learning is appropriate for their organization. Chapter One discusses these foundational concepts and differentiates among four distinct approaches to action learning: the scientific school, the experiential school, the critical reflection school, and the tacit school. Each of these is best applied in particular contexts with the intention of achieving specific learning outcomes. The chapter offers a framework for understanding the current action learning landscape and the implications for practice.

Chapter Two extends this discussion by providing more detail around program designs in the context of the four schools. Chapter Three discusses the learning coach role. It examines a number of issues surrounding this role, including the key competencies that learning coaches require, how the role differs from more traditional group facilitation, and choices around positioning learning coaches in the organization—for example, the use of internal or external learning coaches and the training of coaches.

We next look at the outcomes of action learning applications and highlight the implications for practice. Chapter Four examines how learning transfers from action learning programs to the organizational context. Linking principles of learning transfer from the training literature to action learning program design, it provides examples from two organizations.

Chapter Five provides an example of how action learning can be used for personal development and transformational learning. It offers a detailed example that follows a model closely aligned with the approach of Reg Revans, who is widely regarded as the father of action learning, and looks at how participants experience this kind of action learning program. It also makes the point that transformational learning can be thought of as occurring through successive changes in meaning schemes, not just immediate changes in broader meaning perspectives.

In a sense Chapter Six extends the discussion of learning transfer, focusing on action learning as a vehicle for facilitating transformational culture change. It looks at culture change from a social interaction perspective and identifies components of culture change.

We next summarize the lessons learned and provide additional theory and practices, and sources of information for application. Chapter Seven presents explicit implications for practice, linkages to the learning organization, and suggestions for assessing the learning from action learning programs.

The Appendix provides an annotated lists of resources on action learning.

Our interest is in the use of action learning as a way of producing—through personal, managerial, and organizational learning—organizational change and results. We are particularly interested in the way in which reflection and critical reflection play a role in action learning. Based on that interest, our focus in this book is more on what Chapter One characterizes as the experiential and critical reflection schools of action learning. Our own practice is centered on the critical reflection approach. However, we recognize the importance of a broader understanding of action learning, and the need for taking a "contingency approach" to action learning application. Specifically, the design of an action learning program should be contingent on the learning outcomes desired by management, the culture of the organization, and its tolerance for the ambiguities associated with development and transformation. This book discusses all approaches, just as we have found it necessary to have an appreciation for different approaches in our practice.

Our interest in the critical reflection school rests on the belief that many of the challenges in the future will require the type of learning targeted by this school. Variety in all its forms, the challenges presented to organizations and society by technology, the struggle of individuals to achieve balance among competing priorities in their lives, and the need for collaboration and community in a number of social settings will make this kind learning increasingly important. In this regard, we openly advocate the critical reflection model, although not to the exclusion of the others. As we make clear, the critical reflection approach is not appropriate for all situations, and we provide guidance in deciding which approach to use. We also believe that the dialogue around action learning needs to be expanded to further our understanding of the potential of action learning and development, in terms of both practice and future research into the consequences of different forms of practice. We hope that the ideas we present will stimulate this kind of learning and advance the research agenda as well as practice.

Acknowledgments

We extend special thanks to the reviewers for this book for their many suggestions. Their ideas significantly improved the final product both in the form of those many suggestions incorporated into it and the discussion generated among the editors around those suggestions not adopted. We accept responsibility for the final product, but we have benefited greatly from the work of the reviewers.

We also thank Ernie Turner, Tony Pearson, Sue Lutz, Bob Kolodny, Lars Cederholm, and Chris Dennis for their support, both financial and intellectual, for the research on which parts of this book is based.

Action Reflection Learning and ARL used periodically in this book are registered trademarks of Leadership in International Management, Ltd. (LIM) and are used by permission.

References

Revans, R. (1965). *Science and the manager.* London: Macdonald.

Revans, R. (1971). *Developing effective managers.* New York: Praeger.

Revans, R. (1982). *The origins and growth of action learning.* London: Chartwell-Bratt

Weinstein, K. (1995). *Action learning: A journey in discovery and development.* London: HarperCollins.

Chapter 1

▲ Action Learning
Theoretical Bases and Varieties of Practice

Lyle Yorks
Judy O'Neil
Victoria J. Marsick

The Problem and the Solution. There is never just one way to approach a problem. In action learning, there are four different approaches. Each approach makes different assumptions and tends to produce different results. Knowing the four action learning approaches, their likely results, and the design choices within each will help ensure success.

Susan, a senior human resource development professional working in a large financial services company, experienced a growing sense of confusion as she listened to a consultant talk about action learning. Her company was facing severe pressures from emerging competitors to enter new markets with innovative products and delivery systems. Susan and her colleagues were assessing action learning as a way of developing the capacity for managers and their organization to learn faster and on the fly. They found that the consultant's advice left them more confused than clear about what exactly action learning is! There seemed to be great differences between what they had been reading and what they had just heard.

Shortly after the consultant's visit, two of us met with Susan and her colleagues to discuss how to adapt university courses to meet the company's internal management development needs. As the conversation turned to the relationships among critical thinking, action science, and action learning, a light bulb went off in Susan's head. She realized that there are several different approaches to action learning—differences that are not always clear in the literature. Susan then attended the

International Foundation of Action Learning preconference at the Academy of Human Resource Development and realized that she and her colleagues were talking about very different models of action learning. To move forward, they first needed to think carefully about the outcomes they wished to accomplish. The goals would dictate the action learning approach and program design that would best achieve these outcomes.

Susan's experience is not unique. There is considerable confusion around what action learning is and how it should best be designed and implemented. We wish to answer some questions that we are frequently asked by those who make decisions about whether to adopt action learning:

- How do you define action learning?
- How is your definition different from that of others working in the field?
- Are there different approaches to action learning? If so, what are the implications of these differences for individuals or organizations?
- Does each participant or team of participants have an individual learning agenda?
- What kind of learning outcomes does action learning produce?
- Does action learning require a learning coach? If yes, how does a learning coach differ from a group facilitator?
- How is the effectiveness of an action learning program assessed?
- What articles or books in the action learning literature are important to read?

We write with a point of view: that transformational approaches to action learning have great potential for deep change in people and organizations. However, we also believe that organizations need to match their action learning approach to their readiness level for such changes.

Action Learning Defined

Many different training and learning interventions have been labeled action learning. As Weinstein (1995) notes, the term *action learning* means very different things to various people. Table 1.1 presents several definitions by different researchers. From these definitions, it is apparent that certain principles are common to action learning and distinguish it from other forms of experience-based learning. Its foundation is *working in small groups in order to take action on meaningful problems while seeking to learn from having taken this action.* Some authors add the notion of a cyclical process of taking action, assessing that action through reflection, drawing conclusions, and taking subsequent action based on these conclusions. This cyclical process is critical for certain learning outcomes. Some models also advocate the use of learning coaches, who help learners to question their actions, challenge their assumptions, and commit to meaningful action without offering specific advice. We thus define action learning as follows:

> An approach to working with and developing people that uses work on an actual project or problem as the way to learn. Participants work in small groups to take action to solve their problem and learn how to learn from that action. Often a learning coach works with the group in order to help the members learn how to balance their work with the learning from that work.

All action learning practitioners help people develop new perspectives on challenges they face in their personal and work lives. All cultivate what Reg Revans (1970, 1978), generally regarded as the father of action learning, calls questioning insight.

Action learning is not the same as a case study or experiential programs that elicit principles that are to be subsequently applied in the organization. Also excluded are outdoor adventure experiences such as rappelling and whitewater rafting, or simulation exercises that develop specific instrumental skills. These initiatives do not center on a real work problem in real time.

The distinction between action learning and other forms of experiential learning is important for proper application and assessment. The issue is clarity, not ideological purity. One of us attended a conference designed to help people learn about action learning. Of the many companies presenting, only a few were doing action learning as we have defined it. For example, a bank representative spoke about using work sampling to develop programmed training exercises to train tellers, and an airline spokesperson described its flight simulation program for pilots. The result was confusion for the attendees. If during her initial inquiry into action learning, Susan had attended that conference, she would have been baffled by the array of models presented.

▲ Table 1.1   Definitions of Action Learning

Theorist/Practitioner	Definition
Revans	"Action learning is a means of development, intellectual, emotional or physical that requires its subjects, through responsible involvement in some real, complex and stressful problem, to achieve intended change to improve his observable behavior henceforth in the problem field" (1982, pp. 626–627). "I am often told that managers who discuss their tasks with each other are always doing action learning, or that job rotation is action learning because the managers change factories. I hope that those who study what I have written here will agree that, while action learning may have a little in common with managerial conversation or promotion, it is in practice not identical to either" (1978, p. 3).
McNulty	"Action learning is learning to act through taking action. In its broadest sense, it is a way of tackling complex social and industrial problems which have proven to be of particular value in the development of individual managers" (1979, p. 12).
McGill and Beaty	"Action learning is a continuous process of learning and reflection, supported by colleagues, with an intention of getting things done. Through action learning individuals learn with and from each other by working on real problems and reflecting on their own experiences. The process helps us to take an active stance towards life and helps to overcome the tendency to think, feel and be passive towards the pressures of life" (1992, p. 17).
Pedler	"Action learning is an approach to the development of people in organizations which takes the task as the vehicle for learning. It is based on the premise that there is no learning without action and no sober and deliberate action without learning. On the whole our education

	system has not been based on this principle. The method has been pioneered in work organizations and has three main components—people, who accept the responsibility for taking action on a particular issue; problems, or the tasks that people set themselves; and a set of six or so colleagues who support and challenge each other to make progress on problems. Action learning implies both self-development and organization development. Action on a problem changes both the problem and the person acting upon it. It proceeds particularly by questioning taken-for-granted knowledge" (1991, pp. xxii–xxiii).
Marsick, Cederholm, Turner, and Pearson	"In an Action Reflection Learning program (a form of action learning) the 'training' becomes a project in which learning takes place while participants try to solve a work-related problem. . . . The basic characteristics of an Action Reflection Learning program are: • working in small groups to solve problems • learning how to learn and think critically • building skills to meet the training needs that emerge during a project/problem • developing a participant's own theory of management, leadership, or employee empowerment—a theory that is tested against real-world experiences as well as established tenets" (1992, p. xxx).
Mumford	"Learning for managers should mean learning to take effective action. . . . Learning to take effective action necessarily involves actually taking action, not recommending action or undertaking analysis of someone else's problem. The best form of action for learning is work on a defined project of reality and significance to the managers themselves. . . . The social process is achieved and managed through regular meetings of managers. . . . The role of people providing help for members . . . is essentially and crucially different from that of a normal management teacher. Their role is not to teach . . . but to help the managers learn from exposure to problems and to each other" (1989, p. 2).

Schools of Action Learning Practice

Through an analysis of the various ways action learning is being practiced, O'Neil (1999) identifies four schools of action learning practice: the scientific school, the tacit school, the experiential school, and the critical reflection school. These schools do not represent any preexisting movement of practitioners, and, as with many other typologies, some proponents fit more clearly into one of the schools than do others. Nevertheless, the framework helps to explain variations in practice. At the same time, although the four schools share much in common, their different assumptions regarding learning significantly influence the way in which action learning is practiced. Each of the schools assumes that learning takes place in a different way; each designs activities differently and creates different outcomes. This framework of thinking can help practitioners choose a model based on the learning outcomes they seek and the culture or context within which they are working.

The Scientific School

The scientific school is rooted in the early work of Reg Revans (1970), who drew on his own experiences as a physicist. His approach is highly rational and comes from applying the scientific model to social and workplace problems. Because his work is seminal and elements of it are integrated into the other schools, some detail on his terminology is helpful.

Revans describes his approach to management development as three, interactive systems: Alpha, Beta, and Gamma (MacNamara & Weeks, 1982; Revans, 1970, 1981, 1982, 1987). System Alpha is the structured interplay of three elements of managerial decision making: (1) the manager's value system, (2) the external system that affects the decision being made, and (3) the internal system within which the manager works. System Beta is the negotiation and implementation of that designed strategy. It overlaps with System Alpha in its first steps. System Beta consists of five components (Revans refers to this system by the acronym SHEAR, from the components):

- Survey stage, in which the data for System Alpha are identified
- Hypothesis, a trial decision stage in which one of the alternative designs from System Alpha is selected for experimentation
- Experiment, an action stage in which the trial decision is implemented

- Audit, during which the observed outcome is compared with the expected outcome
- Review, a control stage in which appropriate action is taken on the conclusions reached during the audit stage

Revans (1978) equates the steps of System Beta with the learning process: "recognition, prima facie acceptance, rehearsal, verification, conviction" (p. 14). It places heavy emphasis on the use of data and logical analysis in leading to a thoroughly researched solution, sacrificing immediacy for rightness.

System Gamma involves personal development. It refers to the mental predisposition that a manager brings to the situation. Through continually checking expectations of what should be happening against what is actually happening, the manager identifies discrepancies between his or her first framing of the situation and what subsequent experience suggests was the actual condition. Revans defines learning as the extent to which the manager is able to change perceptions based on this experience. (This is similar to what Cell, 1984, calls situation learning: a change in how one interprets a situation, through either altering one's values or judgment of how things work in a particular situation. It also resembles the discussion in Mezirow, 1991, of learning new meaning schemes, and the concept in Bateson, 1972, of Level II learning, that is, changing the set of alternatives from which one selects actions.)

Revans (1982, 1989) also emphasizes the importance of asking questions, and created a formula to express this: $L = P + Q$ (L = learning, P = programmed instruction, Q = questioning insight). Revans (1989) defines questioning insight as "intuition, things crossing the mind, insight" (p. 102). Pedler (1991) refers to Q as asking discriminating questions. True learning is a combination of this questioning, plus programmed knowledge, P, defined as "the expert knowledge, knowledge in books, what we are told to-do because that is how it has been done for decades" (Weinstein, 1995, p. 44). Questioning opens the manager to new interpretations of experience. Revans (1978) advocates that the following questions be asked at the start of working on a problem:

> "What are we trying to do?"
> "What is stopping us from doing it?"
> "What can we do about it?" [p. 17].

Revans (1978) places importance on learning from peers, whom he calls "comrades in adversity," each wrestling with a difficult, seemingly intractable problem. He is more interested in solving the problem than in the development of interpersonal and leadership competencies. This primary emphasis on the project, coupled with a minimalist role for the "supernumerary" (learning coach), differentiates him from the experiential and critical reflection schools, which emphasize the role of the learning coach and the development of interpersonal, group, and leadership competencies.

The scientific approach is appropriate when the desired outcome is the resolution of problems based on a cautious, data-driven approach centered on reformulating the problem. A second hoped-for outcome is incidental learning around how to continue to learn from one's work and experience. These outcomes are captured by Preston (1977), an executive who participated in a program based on Revans's approach at General Electric Company (GEC):

> Learning, for me, can be classified into two categories. The first involves the learning of facts. The second stems from experience, and fashions the way in which we respond to events in the future. I have learned many facts from my participation in the programme. This was inevitable when undertaking an investigation in depth under such circumstances. I also feel more capable to respond to situations in the future—as a result of the second type of learning—through greater awareness and an understanding of the things that it would be more prudent for me to learn [p. 44].

Casey and Pearce's (1977) discussion of action learning at GEC, from which this quotation is taken, provides a clear, concise case description of this type of program. Written largely by the participants themselves, all of them managers, it offers the successes and struggles of a program based squarely on this school. Foy (1977) has provided another description of the GEC experience; she describes the benefits as "more confident and competent managers, some progress toward resolution to major problems, and, often diffusion of a technique that is useful for gathering information and solving other organizational problems" (p. 167).

The Experiential School

The proponents of this school of action learning base their thinking on Kolb's (1984) experiential learning cycle: having an experience, reflecting on that experience, conceptualizing the experience, and experimenting with the new ideas (Lessem, 1991; McGill & Beaty, 1992; McLaughlin & Thorpe, 1993; Mumford, 1994). Practitioners of this tradition place stronger emphasis than do those in the scientific school on the role of intentional, explicit reflection throughout the process. The learning coach actively designs practices to this end. Group members reflect on experience, followed by action, in order to change, rather than repeat, previous patterns of behavior.

As in the scientific school, practitioners in this school strive for problem reframing and problem solving through situational learning around the project. They develop the ongoing practice of learning from work through learning reviews guided by the learning coach. The experiential school intentionally seeks personal development outcomes by helping people to set and monitor progress toward personal learning goals. The following comments from managers who completed an action learning experience in a large metropolitan utility reflect this emphasis on personal development:

> One of my learning goals is to be a better listener. I am much more patient with my associates. I am getting good results, much better results. I am seeing a real improvement with the attitude of the team.

> One of my teammates asked me a question about my personal learning goal that made me rethink the action I was taking. I'd never thought about it from that perspective. I decided to act on this perspective and got very positive feedback from my coworkers.

Mumford (1993) provides a good introduction to this approach. An example of such an initiative is ARAMARK (Vicere, 1996). Participants reported an increase in self and organizational awareness, collaborative leadership styles, and creative thinking and risk taking. The chief executive officer of ARMARK credits action learning with providing the foundation for the company's growth plan and providing market focus and corporate momentum.

Critical Reflection School

Practitioners in the critical reflection school begin with theories of learning from experience, as does the experiential school, but they differ in how they use reflection (O'Neil, 1999). They believe that reflection must be taken to a deeper level by focusing on underlying premises in the thinking of managers. Mezirow (1991) calls this process critical reflection, through which people recognize that their perceptions are filtered through uncritically accepted views, beliefs, attitudes, and feelings inherited from their own family, school, and society. Such flawed perceptions often distort one's understanding of problems and situations. Senge (1990) describes how these mental models prevent learning in organizations.

Critical reflection in action learning can also go beyond the individual participant's underlying assumptions and can lead to the examination of taken-for-granted organizational norms (Marsick, 1990; Weinstein, 1995) and shared mental models (Senge, 1990). To the extent this is so, it is a tool for examining the deep culture of an organization. Reformulation, reframing, and transformation of the presenting task or project happen when participants uncover misconceptions, norms, and expectations that were often hidden (Marsick & Watkins, 1990; Pedler, 1996; Senge, 1990; Weinstein, 1995).

The goals of this school are personal and organizational transformation. Although guided by strategic intent, the initiatives cannot fully control outcomes because it is expected that they will challenge the status quo. A group in an international foods company, for example, recommended radical restructuring of the company, including the executive team, as a key step toward its project goal of globalization. Both participants and sponsors have to be comfortable with being unsure of the outcomes to adopt this approach. These programs are guided by significant self-direction.

The anticipated outcome of critical thinking programs is breakthrough thinking—the kind that can lead to discontinuous change. An analogy of the impact this kind of change can have is found in what the Fosbury flop did for the performance of high jumpers in track and field. In the Fosbury flop, named after its innovator, the jumper flops backward over the high jump bar. This approach was a complete change from the traditional western roll approach, in which the jumper rolled over the high jump bar with his or her chest facing the bar. When it was introduced, the Fosbury flop looked silly when viewed through the mental models of those accustomed to the traditional approach, but skepticism was soon replaced by total imitation as heretofore resistant world records were convincingly broken by those using the approach.

Another goal of critical reflection programs is generating what Cell (1984) calls transsituation learning: learning how to change one's acts of interpretation through critical reflection on one's own learning processes. This kind of learning is what many learning theorists, including Cell, call learning to learn.

The extent to which critical reflection can be practiced is dependent on the initial tolerance of participants and the organizational cultures in which they function. It is essential that any organization thinking about the critical reflection approach understand that such efforts at generative, transformational learning create extensive noise in the form of questioning long-held sacred cows, along with expressions of discomfort from those individuals who do not want to change (Weinstein, 1995). There is a need for organizational fortitude during the early phases of the process.

The extent to which participants may be prepared to challenge the behavior and thinking of management—thus generating noise in the system—is illustrated by an incident that took place in an international food products company. One participant described what happened when the senior executive team gathered to hear presentations on the projects in the company's first action learning program:

> It was almost laughable in the sense that we'd been through this very intense experience and we met with the clients. We got the senior executives together, and they just basically argued with each other, and started to criticize what people were saying—interrupting them and all. It was said right there that maybe we should spend a little more time with the executive team.

Another comment about the same incident reveals the extent of the transformation that the participants experienced:

> It was such inappropriate behavior, and then I thought, boy, my consciousness has been changed, because I wouldn't have noticed this six months ago. So I think that's important—maybe almost proof of what happened. We had a group of twenty people, and they brought these bulls back into the china shop and they went back to the old, duke-it-out-across-the-boardroom table kind of crap, and it just offended everybody.

Participants confronted the issue immediately with the executive team, and the members of the team responded in a learning way. They did not deny, explode, threaten, or use power that comes with their position to protect themselves. It was the beginning of a process of learning among those at the top of the organization about themselves, about learning, and about change. They began functioning differently, both among themselves and with their subordinates.

An example of the personal development that can take place is taken from the work of Lamm (forthcoming). A senior executive from a global manufacturing company headquartered in Europe comments:

> Before the program, I was convinced I was the owner of truth. After the program I said that nobody ever has the truth. Before I was not listening to others. I have the truth, and I'm to give you the truth. This has been changed. In preparation for decisions, I think it's important now that I have others' points of view and I change.

Descriptions of the critical reflection school are found in Dennis, Cederholm, and Yorks (1996), Marsick (1990), Marsick and Cederholm (1988), and O'Neil, Arnell, and Turner (1996).

Tacit or Incidental School

The tacit school, unlike the other three schools, is distinguished by its lack of specific intentionality toward learning. This difference is most apparent in comparison with the experiential and critical reflection schools, but it is also true for the scientific school. The tacit school assumes that significant learning will take place so long as carefully chosen participants are put together, some team building is done, and information is provided by experts (P learning). Although the program itself is planned, learning is not planned. The learning that does occur is what Marsick and Watkins (1990) have categorized as "incidental" (see, for example, Downham, Noel, & Prendergast, 1992; Noel & Charan, 1988).

In the tacit school, the program focuses primarily on the project itself. Practitioners believe that competencies—for example, in group dynamics, leadership, problem solving, or conflict resolution—are developed in action. The foundation for skills development is laid in the early phase of the program through structured team building and other designed activities in conjunction with information transfer and content learning. This occurs before the action learning teams start gathering data and working on their problems. The teams have logistical support from program administrators, but they do not have learning coaches. Teams do not engage in designed reflection while solving the problem. Accordingly, the tacit school more closely resembles a traditional executive development program linked to a subsequent action project. This school differs from these and other traditional training experiences that incorporate some project work following the training; here the primary emphasis is on doing the project, not putting prior learning into practice. The P learning is preparation for the main event. In traditional training with projects, the learning objectives drive the work experience; in action learning, the project drives the learning experience. However, it is with the tacit school that those traditional training programs incorporating good learning practices often meet at the boundary of action learning.

Tacit action learning programs are used to develop strategic thinking among participants. They tend to reinforce the existing culture and mindset of strong leaders and are appropriate for situations in strong leader or hierarchical cultures in which management wishes to cultivate strategic thinking without questioning organizational norms. Some of the most widely publicized corporate action learning programs, including those at General Electric and TRW, fit into this category.

The Action Learning Pyramid: Making Choices Among Different Programs

Figure 1.1 highlights key similarities and differences among these four schools. We have built an action learning pyramid to help practitioners make choices among different programs based on desired outcomes. We have used the imagery of a pyramid to suggest an accumulative ordering of schools in terms of the kinds of learning that are most likely to be produced and the outcomes desired by the program. As one goes from the bottom of the pyramid to the top, the learning outcomes that can be achieved become more complex, critical, and contextual. This also produces more noise in the system and thus potentially more resistance to the process.

By noise we mean comments challenging the program as participants are asked to reflect on long-held assumptions, mental models, and issues that have been previously treated as givens that are not up for discussion.

▲ **Figure 1.1 Action Learning Pyramid**

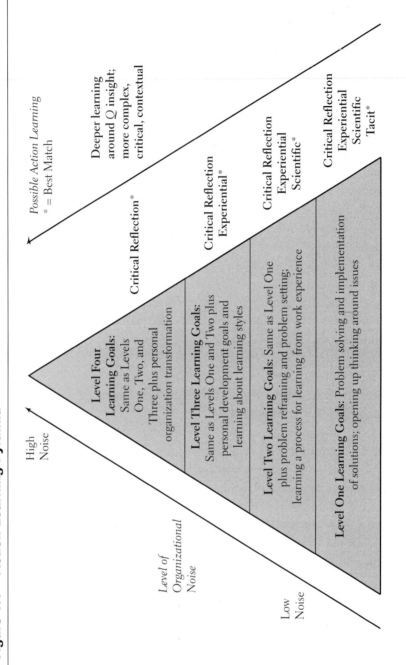

This kind of learning is considerably different from the experience of receiving P learning in a classroom setting, often in an entertaining way. This noise takes on a different character as some participants begin to see a difference in how their project teams are learning and compare this difference with their experience in other groups back in the organization. Practices in the organization become challenged.

At the first level of the pyramid are learning goals centered on problem solving and implementation of solutions for the task or problem. The focus is on strategic issues and developing a strategic business perspective in high-potential executives. All four schools seek to provide this type of learning and appear capable of producing it. However, if this is the primary goal of the program, the tacit approach is probably the best one, especially if management seeks to reinforce a strong existing culture.

The second level of the pyramid reflects learning goals around the task and places emphasis on problem framing and problem posing in addition to problem solving and implementation. It is also expected that participants will gain and subsequently apply skills in learning from their work. The scientific, experiential, and critical reflection schools can deliver this kind of learning. If the goals of the program are limited to this kind of learning, a program approximating Revans's scientific approach may be the best fit.

At the third level of the pyramid, we add explicit goals and outcomes related to personal development, self-knowledge, and learning styles to problem framing, posing, and solving. The experiential and critical reflection schools are more likely than the other two to foster this kind of learning because of the added value of learning coaches and explicit reflection on learning goals around both the task and personal development. Experience has shown that in the absence of a learning coach who explicitly reinforces the goals of the program, learning tends to get driven out by the task focus (O'Neil et al., 1997).

At the fourth level of the pyramid, in addition to learning goals around the task, goals and outcomes include transformational learning for individuals and for building this into the culture of the organization. We believe that the critical reflection school best provides for this kind of learning and culture change. The learning coach fosters a climate in these programs in which participants feel comfortable in examining their beliefs, practices, and norms.

We must add some caveats to our analysis. Because of the differences in program assumptions and design, we believe the potential for fostering transformational learning of a personal nature is greatest in a critical reflection program. However, this kind of learning is in no way ensured. Learning of this developmental kind is not totally predictable or controllable by formula or technique. It is also possible for some people to experience personally transformational learning in tacit programs. Success in achieving transformational outcomes depends to a large extent on the readiness of the learner to confront, rather than resist, the learning experience. It may also depend on the developmental level of the participants in terms of their ability to engage in this kind of transformational learning, although this is certainly a point of debate among learning theorists and researchers. In any case, our own research demonstrates a range of learning outcomes from action learning programs using critical reflection, including resistance. That being said, we also believe that changes in an organizational culture are more likely to be triggered by programs toward the top of the pyramid rather than the bottom, even though such results are no means ensured.

We return, now, to Susan and to the financial services company in which she works. Susan and her colleagues could use the differentiating framework of four schools and the action learning pyramid to decide which ingredients are essential for their program. They can look at their goals to find out which approach will achieve desired outcomes. And they can look at data about the culture of their company and its systems to decide whether their company is able to take advantage of the features of the approach that they wish to implement. The next chapter will help them to make further decisions about the design of their program.

References

Bateson, G. (1972). *Steps to an ecology of the mind.* New York: Ballantine Books.

Casey, D., & Pearce, D. (1977). *More than management development: Action learning at GEC.* Hampshire, England: Gower.

Cell, E. (1984). *Learning to learn from experience.* Albany, NY: State University of New York Press.

Dennis, C. B., Cederholm, L., & Yorks, L. (1996). Learning your way to a global organization. In K. E. Watkins & V. J. Marsick (Eds.), *In action: Creating the learning organization* (pp. 165–153). Alexandria, VA: American Society for Training and Development.

Downham, T. A., Noel, J. L., & Prendergast, A. E. (1992). Executive development. *Human Resource Management, 31*(1&2), 95–107.

Foy, N. (1977). Action learning comes to industry. *Harvard Business Review, 77*(5), 158–168.

Kolb, D. (1984). *Experiential learning.* Englewood Cliffs, NJ: Prentice Hall.

Lamm, S. (forthcoming). *Transformational learning and leadership in context of an action reflection program: A case study in global organization.* Unpublished doctoral dissertation, Teachers College, Columbia University, New York.

Lessem, R. (1991). A biography of action learning. In M. Pedler (Ed.), *Action learning in practice* (2nd ed., pp. 17–30). Brookfield, VT: Gower.

MacNamara, M., & Weekes, W. H. (1982). The action learning model of experiential learning for developing managers. *Human Relations, 35,* 879–902.

Marsick, V. J. (1990). Action learning and reflection in the workplace. In J. Mezirow et al., *Fostering critical reflection in adulthood* (pp. 23–46). San Francisco: Jossey-Bass.

Marsick, V. J., & Cederholm, L. (1988). Developing leadership in international managers—An urgent challenge. *Columbia Journal of World Business, 23*(4), 3–11.

Marsick, V. J., & Watkins, K. E. (1990). *Informal and incidental learning in the workplace.* London: Routledge.

McGill, I., & Beaty, L. (1992). *Action learning: A practitioner's guide.* London: Kogan Page.

McLaughlin, R., & Thorpe, R. (1993). Action learning—A paradigm in emergence: The problems facing a challenge to traditional management education and development. *British Journal of Management, 4*(1), 19–27.

McNulty, N. G. (1979). Management development by action learning. *Training and Development Learning, 32*(3), 12–18.

Mezirow, J. (1991). *Transformative dimensions of adult learning.* San Francisco: Jossey-Bass.

Mumford, A. (1993). *How managers can develop managers.* Brookfield, VT: Gower.

Mumford, A. (1994). A review of action learning literature. *Management Bibliographies and Reviews, 20*(6/7), 2–16.

Noel, J. L., & Charan, R. (1988). Leadership development at GE's Crotonville. *Human Resource Management, 27,* 433–447.

O'Neil, J. (1999). *The role of the learning adviser in action learning.* Unpublished doctoral dissertation, Teachers College, Columbia University, New York.

O'Neil, J., Arnell, E., & Turner, E. (1996). Earning while learning. In K. E. Watkins & V. J. Marsick (Eds.), *In action: Creating the learning organization* (pp. 153–164). Alexandria, VA: American Society for Training and Development.

O'Neil, J., Marsick, V. J., Yorks, L., Nilson, G., & Kolodny, R. (1997). Life on the seesaw: Tensions in action reflection learning. In M. Pedler (Ed.), *Action learning in practice* (3rd ed., pp. 339–346). Brookfield, VT: Gower.

Pedler, M. (1991). Questioning ourselves. In M. Pedler (Ed.), *Action learning in practice* (2nd ed., pp. 63–70). Brookfield, VT: Gower.

Pedler, M. (1996). *Action learning for managers*. London: Lemos & Crane.

Preston, P. (1977). Learning how to learn. In D. Casey & D. Pearce (Eds.), *More than management development: Action learning at GEC* (pp. 40–44). Aldershot, England: Gower.

Revans, R. W. (1970). The managerial alphabet. In G. Heald (Ed.). *Approaches to the study of organizational behavior*. London: Tavistock.

Revans, R. W. (1978). *The a. b. c. of action learning: A review of 25 years of experience*. Salford, England: University of Salford.

Revans, R. W. (1981). The nature of action learning. *Omega*, 9(1), 9–24.

Revans, R. W. (1982). *The origin and growth of action learning*. London: Chartwell Bratt.

Revans, R. W. (1987). International perspectives on action learning. *Manchester Training Handbooks*. Manchester: IDPM Publications.

Revans, R. W. (1989). *The golden jubilee of action learning*. Manchester, England: Manchester Action Learning Exchange, University of Manchester.

Senge, P. M. (1990). *The fifth discipline: The art and practices of the learning organization*. New York: Doubleday/Currency.

Vicere, A. A. (1996). Executive education: The leading edge. *Organizational Dynamics*, pp. 67–81.

Weinstein, K. (1995). *Action learning: A journey in discovery and development*. New York: HarperCollins.

Chapter 2

Issues in the Design and Implementation of an Action Learning Initiative

Judy O'Neil
Robert L. Dilworth

The Problem and the Solution. Action learning does not just happen automatically and can spin out of control just like any other initiative. Action learning initiatives must be purposefully designed and implemented. This chapter covers basic issues such as designing individual and team projects, timing, and kinds of structured learning in relation to the four approaches to action learning.

Once an organization makes a decision about a potential action learning school, there are a number of design decisions that need to be made in order to move forward with the action learning initiative. As with any other organizational initiative, of course, it is necessary to determine the specific needs that are going to be addressed. A good needs assessment is important for action learning design work and can be accomplished using the traditional means (O'Neil, Foy, Bailey, & Cuozzo, 1995; Rothwell & Kazanas, 1992).

The intent of the needs assessment is to determine the gaps that should be addressed among the existing competencies of participants and organizational needs as articulated in the company's vision, strategy, and other statements of intent in the action learning initiative. This assessment can be performed using many methods. Interviews with senior-level managers, potential participants, and their managers are frequently used. There may be useful data from previous organizational surveys or studies. For example, in the international food company program discussed in Chapter One, the action learning program was preceded by, among other things, a corporate cultural survey and interviews that identified a gap between the intention of becoming a global organization and the reported sets of competencies and cultural characteristics of the existing organization (Yorks, O'Neil, Marsick, Nilson, & Kolodny, 1996). Based on these data, the program staff developed the themes of the program, identified certain kinds of structured learning inputs (P learning in terms introduced in Chapter One), and took these needs into consideration in facilitating reflection throughout the program.

There are also some specific action learning considerations—for example:

- Should the problems worked on be ones that are of a familiar or an unfamiliar nature?
- Should the initiative take place in a familiar or an unfamiliar setting?
- Should the problems be group or individual projects?
- How will participants be chosen?
- How much time will the participants and the organization be willing to invest in the initiative?
- Will P (content) learning be provided, and if so, what and how?

This chapter addresses these questions while providing guidance in making these basic design decisions. In addition, we discuss the issue of codesign and provide some thoughts on implementation.

Problems and Settings

A good place to start these considerations is with Revans. Revans (1983) points out that we are confronted with two types of problems, unfamiliar or familiar; the same dichotomy—unfamiliar or familiar—applies also to the setting in which participants are placed for an action learning program. Revans refers to the resulting two-by-two model as exchange options (see Figure 2.1). Thinking of design choices in the context of the model highlights issues that arise with each cell.

If the program is designed around a familiar problem in a familiar setting (cell I), the group dynamics will tend to be predictable. Individual participants may have worked together before; they may even be a natural

▲ Figure 2.1   Revans's Model of Exchange Options

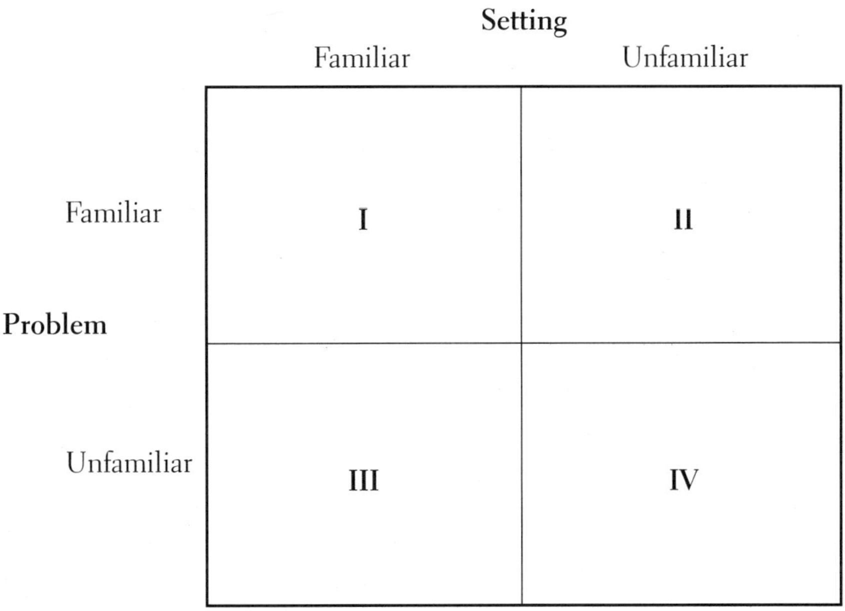

	Setting Familiar	Setting Unfamiliar
Problem Familiar	I	II
Problem Unfamiliar	III	IV

team. One of the potential problems with this mix is that learning might be limited to existing patterns of thinking, which reemerge in the group. The group can easily fall into a pattern of traditional problem-solving activity. For example, a large utility in the Northeast has an action learning initiative, ongoing for over two years, that is bringing about change and transformation in the organization. One of the earlier teams was an intact work group addressing a work-related problem. The participants thought at first that their familiarity with one another and the project would be of benefit to them. Instead they quickly recognized the difficulty they had in trying to think about the project in new ways and decided to nominate one of the participants as a devil's advocate whose role it would be to challenge the team's thinking.

The presence of a learning coach to encourage questioning insight can help in overcoming this problem through open dialogue to develop new dynamics. Programs involving familiar programs in familiar settings best adopt an approach similar to the scientific or the experiential school since the learning coach can overcome some of the learning limitations that can emerge. Typically companies pursuing this option are not trying to accomplish transformative learning outcomes and want learning that is more focused on personal development than organizational change.

The opposite end of the spectrum of design choices from cell I involves placing people in an unfamiliar setting to work on an unfamiliar problem or issue (cell IV). Participants in this design option, especially in a large company, may not even know each other beforehand. Revans argues that this kind of action learning design promises the deepest learning experience. His reasoning is that the design places people farthest out of their comfort zone and distances them from their experience and expertise. Therefore, they must ask fresh questions.

This option fits with any of the schools and is a particularly good fit with the critical reflection school. The unfamiliarity of both setting and problem helps make the job of a learning coach easier since there is an open environment for questioning and challenging of assumptions. However, this approach tends to produce significant noise in the organization. Also, management needs to be prepared for outcomes that may be both unanticipated and unintended. It is very important that organizational leadership understand the generative potential of the process and be supportive of the effort. This support goes beyond simple endorsement; top management must become actively engaged with the initiative.

A large southern utility company created a team in the late 1980s to address a persistent power generation problem that had resisted correction for several years. The team members were drawn from various areas of the company to work in an area unfamiliar to them, and they had never previously addressed a problem of the type involved. They solved the problem, probably because they went outside the boundaries of established practice.

Revans's "Belgium model" is another example (1983). In the 1960s, five top executives, each from an entirely different industry, were brought together in Belgium. The executives were then each assigned an individual problem of great complexity and importance in an industry far removed from their own area of expertise. The result was a number of generative solutions to their problems.

Placing people in an unfamiliar setting to examine a familiar problem (cell II) can also generate fresh questions. This option can be used with all the action learning schools. Since the outcomes can challenge existing structures and norms, this option can benefit an organization interested in bringing about organizational change. Participants also have the opportunity to establish networks and develop through experience with a different part of the organization.

Some years ago, the ten largest London hospitals, in what Revans refers to as the Hospital Internal Communication (HIC) Study, banded together to explore problems of common concern. However, rather than examine the problems in their own hospitals, teams were exchanged. By examining a familiar problem in an unfamiliar place, the teams arrived at new ways of problem resolution. As shown in the evaluation, the changes instituted resulted in, among other things, shorter hospital stays, reduced patient mortality rates, and increased employee morale (Coghill & Stewart, 1998, p. 36).

The final cell (III) involves working on an unfamiliar problem in a familiar setting. This option can also be used with any of the schools. With its focus in a familiar setting, it is an especially good choice for the experiential school, with its emphasis on personal development, since participants can easily be with a peer group with whom they can develop personal learning goals and provide ongoing feedback. This option, like the previous two, carries with it implications for organizational change, since working with an unfamiliar problem will generate new, fresh questions.

An example from the management experience of one of us (R.D.) describes a major computer problem that existed in a large organization and had resisted repeated attempts at correction. A team was assembled from across the organization. Few of the individuals on the team had any real computer experience, yet they quickly solved the problem, attributing resolution to the fact that they were "not blocked by prior knowledge" (what in Revans's parlance is called P, for programmed instruction). The team members found that the solution required the assembly of a number of individual changes, few of which had been thought about previously.

A second example from our experience involves the initiative within a northeast utility where projects are being drawn directly from the organization's business plan. Supervisors and managers are asked to address issues their company is facing (familiar setting) that are more broad ranging and complex (unfamiliar problem) than any they have tried to solve before.

Choosing an appropriate exchange option is important. There have been instances of companies' adopting one of the more expansive forms of action learning (say, unfamiliar problem in an unfamiliar setting), only to find it necessary to pull back quickly. In one of these situations, the leadership team in the company had supported the process and told the workforce that they would be empowered to implement their recommendations. The workforce took top leadership at its word and proceeded to recommend major changes. This unanticipated outcome unnerved the company leadership, who stopped the initiative. This decision carried a heavy price. The workforce in this situation tended to be unreceptive to future efforts at mobilizing their energy.

The problem was not with the action learning per se but rather with the option chosen. Corporate leaders were not fully aware of the potential for unanticipated outcomes and became unwilling to follow through on their expressed commitment to accept the learning from the process they had initiated.

Group or Individual Projects

Another important design issue is whether to have a group address a project they have in common or have each participant bring his or her own project to the group. Action learning works effectively in both instances. As with other design choices, which one is selected depends on the goals of the effort and the organizational context.

There are some basic framing criteria for all action learning projects, both group and individual. In addition to being based in the real work of the organization, action learning projects usually meet the following criteria:

- They are complex, overarching, and often cross-functional (Marsick & Watkins, 1992; O'Neil & Marsick, 1994).
- They are problems, opportunities, or difficulties about which "different reasonable, experienced and honest men would wish to pursue different courses of action" (Revans, 1978, p. 11), and there is no single solution (Weinstein, 1995).
- They are actual problems, meaningful to participants, and about which participants have the motivation to act (McGill & Beaty, 1992; O'Neil & Marsick, 1994; Weinstein, 1995).

When a group has a common problem on which to focus, it is usually an organizational problem, and there is often a problem owner or sponsor outside the group who takes on the responsibility for supporting implementation. Individual problems belong to the participant; although they can also be sponsored, often they are not. They can be either organizationally related or personal projects.

When participants work on a group project, the intent usually is to work on it for the development of organizational goals. Although personal development can also be addressed in the design, the focus is on the organization (McGill & Beaty, 1992). A caution with group projects is the danger of the group's focusing too much on the project work and becoming a task force—focusing on simply solving the problem at the expense of any learning. In an action learning initiative for Volvo Truck, participants felt that more of a balance was needed between the project and learning. One participant stated, "I think that the project work part consumes too much in relation to the real learning of it" (Arnell, 1995, p. 4).

A group project can be part of the design in any of the schools; it is frequently found in the critical reflection school and is always used in the tacit school. Any of the options mentioned in the previous section can use a group project, but a group project is particularly appropriate for an unfamiliar problem in an unfamiliar setting. In the northeast utility company's program, teams work on a common project drawn from the organization's business plan and sponsored by a manager outside the team. A number of descriptions of how groups work together on a common project can be found in special issues on action learning in *Performance Improvement Quarterly* (for example, Dilworth, 1998) and in O'Neil, Arnell, and Turner (1996).

Individual projects can also be part of the design for any of the schools, except the tacit, which involve company programs centered around team projects sponsored by executives who are seeking answers to questions. Individual projects are most often used in the experiential and scientific schools. When participants have their own individual projects, there is a greater focus on personal development (Mumford, 1995). There is also a greater opportunity for implementation of the outcome of the action learning process. Those who favor the use of individual projects contend that for the action learning process itself to be effective, the participants must follow through to implementation. This is considered necessary to induce a true sense of ownership. CONOCO's "Learning Labs" bring together individuals working on independent projects within their parent organizations. (For a good description of how groups work on individual projects, see Weinstein, 1995.)

Choosing Participants and Forming Groups

Referred to as "comrades in adversity" by Revans (1982) and "fellows in opportunity" by Mumford (1996), the first criteria for choosing participants are the objectives and intent of the initiative. For example, in an action learning program at an international food company, since an objective was to create a global organization, participants were chosen from the ranks of upper management (Dennis, Cederholm, & Yorks, 1996). At the northeastern utility company previously referred to, the intent is to develop all levels of management to function successfully in a competitive environment, so participants are chosen from supervisors through senior-level executives. The company has also included some bargaining unit employees depending on the project.

Once the participants have been identified, the next important element is to form groups based on the greatest diversity possible. Diversity is considered important because a variety of perspectives enhance learning and a greater mix of participants leads to more creative problem solutions. Diversity refers to differences in background, work experience, age, gender, nationality, and, where known, learning style differences and personality mix. An effort should be made to not include people who are considered to be subject matter experts on the project. This helps to avoid the "expert solution" that Revans (1982) warns practitioners about.

The ideal group size is considered to be five to seven participants. This size provides for diversity of perspectives and permits full participation. With group projects, this size allows for meaningful team dynamics. With individual projects, five to seven participants allows each participant to have a reasonable amount of time—also referred to as airspace—to address his or her problem within a one-day meeting time, which is the norm.

A final consideration in choosing participants is whether participation should be voluntary. Many action learning practitioners believe that participants should be volunteers. Some initiatives use an introductory session to educate potential participants on the action learning process. In O'Neil's study (1999), a participant explained, "The ground rule I suggest is that they can come along to this two or three hours with no obligation to join a group. After that meeting, somebody in the company collects the names of people who want to be involved." This philosophy can run into problems when the organization is using the initiative for development or change, and feels that it is necessary for certain employees to attend. In these cases, the design may need to address the issues of uncertainty and resistance.

In the utility company program, the objective is to help all supervisors and managers change and transform the way they do their work, so the organization decided not to have the program be voluntary. The design of the program includes strong sponsor support for both the projects and the learning that participants gain from the project. Sponsors choose participants for their teams and call each participant in advance to explain why he or she has been chosen and what he or she will bring to the team. In that initial telephone call and throughout the initiative, they stress the importance of both the task and learning from the task.

Once this selection process has been made a half-day orientation meeting is scheduled. An important activity at this orientation is a session with a panel of previous participants who describe what the action learning experience was like for them and what the new participants can anticipate getting out of it. Participants have described this discussion with peers as very helpful.

In another nonvoluntary program, executives nominate potential participants according to criteria developed by the program director that reflect the organization's development needs. The program director makes a final selection, usually in consultation with the executives making the nomination.

Generally nonvoluntary programs are initiated in response to specific organizational needs around organizational change and management development. To be excluded from such programs in this context is career limiting; thus, as long as the programs are perceived by the organization as strongly supported by top management, participants want to be selected.

Time and Spacing of the Initiative

The amount of time for an action learning initiative varies widely, depending on the chosen school, organizational needs, and the amount of time the organization is willing to invest in the initiative. In some designs, participants meet one day at a time over the course of several months (McGill & Beaty, 1995; Weinstein, 1995). In other designs groups meet for several days at a time, spread out over several months (Dennis, Cederholm, & Yorks, 1996; O'Neil, Arnell, & Turner, 1996), and in yet other designs the groups meet for several days but just once (Noel & Charan, 1988).

Tables 2.1 through 2.4 provide examples of designs for each of the schools. The learning goals of the scientific school in Table 2.1 emphasize both problem solving and problem reframing as well as learning a process for learning from work experience. This design is based on Revan's original program. It took place over a time span of nine months to a year. The individual project belonged to, or was owned by, both a client and sponsor from each of the nineteen participating organizations.

The learning goals of the experiential school in Table 2.2 emphasize personal development, as well as problem framing and problem solving. Here the time span is six months. Participants from the same or different organizations own their individual projects. The learning goals of the critical reflection school in Table 2.3 emphasize personal and organizational transformation, as well as personal development, problem reframing, and problem solving. This design takes five to six months; it is a group project owned by the client or sponsor, and all participants are from the same organization. Finally, Table 2.4 shows an action learning design for the tacit school. Here the learning goals emphasize problem solving. This is a four-week group project owned by the client or sponsor, with all participants from the same organization.

Although the length of programs and spacing of days within them varies, research shows that groups need to meet often enough to ensure continuity of the process (McNamara, 1996). McNamara found that if groups met less frequently than once a month, the participants tended to lose momentum and trust. Data gathered as part of the program assessment in the northeastern public utility company showed that teams needed to meet for two consecutive days each time they met in order to be able to address both projects and personal development.

Having the time with the group extend over a period of time is important in the experiential and critical reflection schools for a couple of reasons. First, having an extended time to meet is linked with the importance of having the time to take action, and therefore bringing about cycles of

▲ Table 2.1   Action Learning Design for the Scientific School

Timing	Content
1 month	Introductory course that covered economic theory, systems, communications, and learning. Assignment of participants to project in organization other than their own.
3–4 months	Spent in project organization and diagnosing the problem. One day a week in small group discussing projects and progress. May receive support from learning adviser. Consultation with academics at Harvard and MIT for testing or proposed recommendations.
3–4 months	Spent in project organization securing acceptance of recommendations and initiating implementation. Regular small group meetings. May receive support from learning adviser.

Sources: Casey & Pearce (1977); McNulty (1979).

action and reflection. Second most learning coaches try to transfer the skills they use with a group to the group participants. The extended time is needed to be able to achieve at least some measure of the transfer of learning coach skills to the group. When a program has a time span of nine months or more, as in many designs in the scientific school, the ability of the coach to make himself or herself redundant is greatly increased.

These time demands seemingly run counter to pressures in organizations for shorter training designs and problem-solving time frames. All things being equal, any program must be run as efficiently as possible in terms of time and resources without sacrificing effectiveness. However, two factors must be kept in mind relative to the issue of the time demands of action learning. First, action learning programs are generally targeted toward intensive development along a number of dimensions while working on relatively difficult problems. They are not put in place to meet relatively routine, though important, needs in these areas. It is by no means clear that this level of development and problem solving is achieved as effectively by shorter investments in time. In practice, many of the problems worked on in action learning programs are highly challenging ones that the organizations have not been able to resolve through alternative

▲ Table 2.2 **Action Learning Design for the Experiential School**

Timing	Content
Week 1 1 day	Introduction to basic concepts of action learning. Begin work on individual projects. Each participant given "airspace" to discuss project. Group uses a questioning-based process with support from learning coach. Participants revisit project and assess what they are learning at regular intervals. Just-in-time learning provided by learning coach as needed.
Week 4 1 day	Each participant given "airspace" to discuss project. Group uses a questioning-based process with support from learning coach. Participants revisit project and assess what learning is occurring at regular intervals. Just-in-time learning provided by learning coach as needed.
Week 7 1 day	Each participant given "airspace" to discuss project. Group uses a questioning-based process with support from learning coach. Participants revisit project and assess what learning is occurring at regular intervals. Just-in-time learning provided by learning coach as needed.
Week 10 1 day	Each participant given "airspace" to discuss project. Group uses a questioning-based process with support from learning coach. Participants revisit project and assess what learning is occurring at regular intervals. Just-in-time learning provided by learning coach as needed.
Week 13 1 day	Each participant given "airspace" to discuss project. Group uses a questioning-based process with support from learning coach. Participants revisit project and assess what learning is occurring at regular intervals. Just-in-time learning provided by learning coach as needed.
Week 17 1 day	Each participant given "airspace" to discuss project. Group uses a questioning-based process with support from learning coach. Participants revisit project and assess what learning is occurring at regular intervals. Just-in-time learning provided by learning coach as needed.

Week 21 1 day	Each participant given "airspace" to discuss project. Group uses a questioning-based process with support from learning coach. Participants revisit project and assess what learning is occurring at regular intervals. Just-in-time learning provided by learning coach as needed.
Week 25 1 day	Each participant given "airspace" to discuss project. Group uses a questioning-based process with support from learning coach. Participants revisit project and assess what learning is occurring at regular intervals. Just-in-time learning provided by learning coach as needed.
Week 29 1 day	Each participant given "airspace" to discuss project. Group uses a questioning-based process with support from learning coach. Participants revisit project and assess what learning is occurring at regular intervals. Just-in-time learning provided by learning coach as needed.
Week 33 1 day	Each participant given "airspace" to discuss project. Group uses a questioning-based process with support from learning coach. Participants revisit project and assess what learning is occurring at regular intervals. Just-in-time learning provided by learning coach as needed.

Sources: Bourner & Weinstein (1996); Weinstein (1995).

means. Second, generally the purpose of action learning is accomplishing both problem resolution and development, a task more complex than attempting either in isolation of the other. The argument for action learning is that dealing with this complexity is worth the investment because action learning is a highly effective means of accomplishing both objectives.

Programmed Learning

Any programmed (P) learning is determined based on the school and what the organization wants to achieve as a result of the initiative. The designs in Tables 2.1 through 2.4 give some examples of P learning for each school. In the example for the scientific school in Table 2.1, the design calls for specific P to be provided within the structure of a supporting

▲ Table 2.3 Action Learning Design for the Critical Reflection School

Timing	Content
Week 1—6 days	Groups formed and assigned projects. P instruction provided around theme for the week: leadership. Groups work on project with support by learning adviser. Just-in-time learning provided by learning adviser. Groups present recommendations to client or sponsor.
5–6 weeks	Participants return to job and continue some work on project. May meet with group without learning adviser.
Week 2—6 days	Groups formed and assigned projects. P instruction provided around theme for the week: personal development. Groups work on project with support by learning adviser. Just-in-time learning provided by learning adviser. Groups present recommendations to client or sponsor.
5–6 weeks	Participants return to job and continue some work on project. May meet with group without learning adviser.
Week 3—6 days 5–6 weeks	Participants return to job and continue some work on project. May meet with group without learning adviser.
Week 4—6 days	P instruction provided around theme for the week: communication. Groups work on project with support by learning adviser. Just-in-time learning provided by learning adviser. Groups present recommendations to client or sponsor.

Source: Dennis, Cederholm, & Yorks (1996).

▲ **Table 2.4 Action Learning Design for the Tacit School**

Week	Topics
1	Programmed (P) instruction on topics that support the objectives and intent of the initiative—strategy, globalization Leadership Development Team Building
2	Programmed (P) instruction on topics that support the objectives and intent of the initiative Leadership Development Team Building Introduction to Action Learning Projects
3	Teams work on action learning projects at business site
4	Presentation of recommendations for action learning projects Team and individual development, feedback, and action plans
6–8 months later	Follow-up

Source: Noel & Charan (1988).

academic setting (Casey & Pearce, 1977) at the start of the program. The content was predetermined to meet the issues the participants would encounter in working on their projects. In the example for the experiential school in Table 2.2, there is little preset P other than the introduction to action learning. What P is delivered is done as just-in-time learning—information that is identified and requested by the group as it is needed. This is provided by the learning coach, a participant, or, if needed, an outside resource (McGill & Beatty, 1995; Pedler, 1996; Weinstein, 1995).

The critical reflection example in Table 2.3 calls for the learning coach to provide both P and just-in-time learning, although this design also makes use of outside resources as needed to address the various topics (Dennis, Cederholm, & Yorks, 1996). Each week is designed to address the specific objectives determined through the earlier needs assessment in the organization. In the tacit school example in Table 2.4, the P is preset and provided by outside experts (Noel & Charan, 1988).

Codesign of the Initiative

A strength of action learning is in its adaptability. To work properly, it must match with both the corporate culture and the issues and objectives to be addressed. There is no universal method or one-size-fits-all approach. Based on this, codesign between the action learning consultants (either internal or external) and the organization for which the action learning initiative is intended is very important.

In terms of codesign, the northeastern utility company serves as a good example. In moving to an action learning approach for organizational transformation and leadership development, the company went through various stages. The initial design was created between the external consultants and internal human resource professional. After the pilot, human resources and line management established corporate processes to support the initiative, with top management articulating and leading the effort with strong external consultant support.

An advisory team was formed in the company consisting of associates from different groups within the organization. Their responsibilities included recommending projects and sponsors. They kept the program as a work in process through the use of program evaluation data to plan future strategy and direction of the program. By fall 1998, eight major action learning initiatives had been conducted, each involving four action learning groups. The sponsors of the action learning teams and projects had previously undergone the action learning experience directly. Therefore, when they worked with a team, they operated with empathy and firsthand knowledge of the dynamics. It also allowed them to blend easily with the learning coach (an external consultant) who was working with a team. Each action learning experience at the utility builds on what went before it. The implementation design has undergone continuous evolution in the process.

Implementation Considerations

There are two levels in implementation that need to be anticipated and understood in order to ensure a successful initiative: the level of the participant and the level of the initiative.

Table 2.5 Outcomes of Action Learning Interventions

"Nutrients" That Support Success	"Killers" That Contribute to Failure
Top leadership acts in accordance with the intent, objectives, and values of the initiative	Top leadership is not committed
The people in power and influence makers learn and change	The intervention is not interrelated with the system
The environment is one of trust, not one of fear	Risks and mistakes are not tolerated
The intervention engages participants' hearts, heads, and guts	There is inconsistent, part-time participation
The organization and intervention support authentic behavior in line with participants' values and beliefs	The intervention is seen as a passing fad
The initiative maximizes and respects diversity of all kinds through the mix of participants	People who do not conform to the "right" corporate image are excluded
Projects are built around real tasks of importance to the organization and individual	Projects are not seen as important to the organization and individual
The design team and participants are clear about the process and purpose of the intervention, and design the initiative accordingly	The intervention is seen as separate events, instead of steps in a process and strategically linked
The organization expects changes throughout the process	Key players do not understand the process and do not take the time to reflect, evaluate, redesign, and renew.

Source: Adapted from O'Neil & Marsick (1994). *Original source:* © 1993 by Institute for Leadership in International Management, Ltd.

For the participant level, it is necessary to anticipate the rhythms of the learning process. At the start, participants can be extremely uncomfortable. They typically ask, "What is this really about?" "When will someone lay out the specific agenda we are to follow?" Some participants require a great deal of structure and have trouble coping when they do not get it. The tension between task completion and learning can create conflict among participants and between participants and the learning coach role (O'Neil et al., 1997). At the middle stage of an initiative, most action learning groups hit some form of stride, but as the end approaches, self-doubts can begin to reassert themselves as participants wonder, "Will we really be able to get this pulled together and presented in time?"

In schools that use learning coaches, this situation can present a great challenge. There can be great temptation for the learning coach to bail a group out. A group may press the coach for interventions that ease their concerns by providing solution options to consider. There can be a desire on the part of the group to reestablish a dependency relationship with the sponsor. At that point, participants and program staff need to trust the process. If the process has been set in motion properly at the beginning, the outcomes will be those that are desired.

The principles set out in Table 2.5 show which action learning interventions support success and which contribute to failure. (Other stories of factors that contribute to success and failure of action learning initiatives can be found in Inglis, 1994, pp. 167–186, and Weinstein, 1995, pp. 284–290.)

References

Arnell, E. (1995). *Volvo Truck Management Program VTM 5 Evaluation, Summary of results, Part 2: Qualitative data.* Unpublished company report.

Casey, D., & Pearce, D. (1977). *More than management development: Action learning at GEC.* Hampshire, England: Gower.

Coghill, N., & Stewart, J. (1998). *The NHS: Myth, monster, or service—Action learning in a hospital.* Salford, England: Revans Centre for Action Learning and Research.

Dennis, C. B., Cederholm, L., & Yorks, L. (1996). Learning your way to a global organization. In K. E. Watkins & V. J. Marsick (Eds.), *In action: Creating the learning organization* (pp. 165–177). Alexandria, VA: American Society for Training and Development.

Dilworth, R. L. (Ed.). (1998). Special issue on action learning. *Performance Improvement Quarterly, 11*(1).

Inglis, S. (1994). *Making the most of action learning.* Brookfield, VT: Gower.

Marsick, V. J., & Watkins, K. E. (1992). *Informal and incidental learning in the workplace.* London: Routledge.

McGill, I., & Beaty, L. (1992). *Action learning: A practitioner's guide.* London: Kogan Page.

McNamara, C. (1996). *Evaluation of a group-managed, multi-technique management development program that includes action learning.* Unpublished doctoral dissertation, Graduate School of the Union Institute, Minneapolis, Minnesota.

Mumford, A. (1995). Learning in action. *Industrial and Commercial Training, 27*(8), 36–40.

Mumford, A. (1996). Effective learners in action learning sets. *Employee Counseling Today, 8*(6), 5–12.

Noel, J. L., & Charan, R. (1988). Leadership development at GE's Crotonville. *Human Resource Management,* pp. 433–447.

O'Neil, J. A. (1999). *The role of the learning advisor in action learning.* Unpublished dissertation, Teachers College, Columbia University, New York.

O'Neil, J., Arnell, E., & Turner, E. (1996). Earning while learning. In K. E. Watkins & V. J. Marsick (Eds.), *In action: Creating the learning organization* (pp. 153–164). Alexandria, VA: American Society for Training and Development.

O'Neil, J., Foy, N., Bailey, C., & Cuozzo, P. (1995). A best practices: Program development model. *Adult Learning, 7*(2), 20–22.

O'Neil, J., & Marsick, V. J. (Fall 1994). Becoming critically reflective through action reflection learning. In A. Brooks & K. Watkins (Eds.), *The emerging power of action learning technology* (pp. 17–30). New Directions for Adult and Continuing Education, no. 63. San Francisco: Jossey-Bass.

O'Neil, J., Marsick, V. J., Yorks, L., Nilson, G., & Kolodny, R. (1997). Life on the seesaw: Tensions in action reflection learning. In M. Pedler (Ed.), *Action learning in practice* (3rd ed., pp. 339–346). London: Gower.

Revans, R. W. (1978). *The a. b. c. of action learning: A review of 25 years of experience.* Salford, England: University of Salford.

Revans, R. W. (1982). *The origin and growth of action learning.* London: Chartwell Bratt.

Revans, R. W. (1983). Action learning projects. In B. Taylor & G. Lippitt (Eds.), *Management development and training handbook* (2nd ed., pp. 226–274). New York: McGraw-Hill.

Rothwell, W. J., & Kazanas, H. C. (1992). *Mastering the instructional design process.* San Francisco: Jossey-Bass.

Weinstein, K. (1995). *Action learning: A journey in discovery and development.* New York: HarperCollins.

Yorks, L., O'Neil, J., Marsick, V. J., Nilson, G. E., & Kolodny, R. (1996). Boundary management in action reflection learning research: Taking the role of a sophisticated barbarian. *Human Resource Development Quarterly, 7*(4), 313–329.

Chapter 3

Facilitating Action Learning
The Role of the Learning Coach

Judy O'Neil

> ***The Problem and the Solution.*** The HRD professional must move from the role of trainer to the role of learning coach in order to achieve success through action learning. This is not a simple shift. This chapter clearly defines the role of learning coach and illustrates the specific tasks required to succeed.

Although the role of the learning coach (also referred to in the literature as set adviser, learning adviser, and project team adviser) is prominent in the action learning literature, no one has systematically defined the role. Knowledgeable practitioners have written about the learning coach role from their personal experience. Understandably, these writers describe the role according to their espoused school of action learning, their personal skill mix, and their view of how the learning coach should support the kind of learning they believe takes place in action learning (McGill & Beaty, 1992; O'Neil & Marsick, 1994; Revans, 1978). The result is that the same confusion surrounding the definition of action learning confronts people seeking to understand the learning coach role.

This chapter primarily looks at the variations of the learning coach role across the experiential and critical reflection approaches and highlights implications for practice. These are the two schools in which the learning coach plays a continuing role in the learning process. In the scientific school, the learning coach is primarily viewed as being involved in initiating—or starting up—an action learning group. In this role, the coach's activities in the scientific school are very similar to those in the experiential and critical reflection schools. The tacit school does not have a formal learning coach role.

The chapter draws heavily on recent research into the learning coach role involving extensive interviews with a large number of prominent action learning practitioners in all three schools and systematic field observation (O'Neil, 1999). A great deal of common agreement about the learning coach role exists across the experiential and critical reflection schools. The principal differences are found in the form of reflective interventions that are made in the two schools.

Learning Coach or Not?

The role of the learning coach is considered important to the action learning process by many practitioners but not all. The disagreement as to whether the learning coach is always required has its foundation in the work of Revans. Revans (1991) argues that the learning coach role should be limited to the start of an action learning program to ensure that managers understand that they have the ability to learn from one another but that the ongoing support of the learning coach is unnecessary. He believes that the ability to learn from experience is latent in managers, and in time and given real work, it will emerge of its own accord, so the need for a learning coach to help that learning take place is unnecessary. He also has an inherent distrust of experts and considers learning coaches as another form of expert (Revans, 1978).

Many other action learning practitioners, however, see the role of the learning coach as necessary. "Although it is theoretically possible, we know of few examples where action learning groups operate without coaches" (Pedler, 1991, p. 291). Some of the reasons given in support of the learning coach role include disagreement with the idea of latent learning skills and insufficient time in most programs for those skills to emerge if they do exist (Bourner & Weinstein, 1996). Although these writers disagree with Revans over the need for an ongoing learning coach, they agree with him that it is important that the coach not take on the role of the expert and teach. The coach's activities should instead focus on helping participants to learn the skills necessary for helping one another learn from their experience (Bourner & Weinstein, 1996; Inglis, 1994; Lawlor, 1991; Lawrence, 1991; McGill & Beaty, 1995; Mumford, 1992; Pedler, 1991; Weinstein, 1995).

The literature describes a variety of roles of the learning coach (Casey, 1991; Harries, 1991; Marsick, 1990; Marsick & Watkins, 1990;

McGill & Beaty, 1992; O'Neil & Marsick, 1994; Pedler, 1991): supporter, reflector, challenger, questioner, and mirror of the group's values, expectations, norms, and beliefs. Learning coaches help participants learn through balancing the tension between the project and learning from the project (O'Neil et al., 1997). This is accomplished through a variety of interventions and just-in-time learning to help create situations for learning.

Background of Learning Coaches

In order to make an informed decision regarding the use of a learning coach and to choose the appropriate resource to fill the role, it is important to understand more about the learning coach. We start by looking at the kind of individual who would play the role.

There are as many views in the literature on the appropriate background for a learning coach as there are views about the role itself (O'Neil, 1997). One area of agreement is that learning coaches are not necessarily drawn from a human resource background. Rather, there are many and varied backgrounds that a person can draw from in order to be able to perform as a learning coach (O'Neil, 1997). In a group in Sweden, for example, the coaches come from diverse backgrounds including doctors, lawyers, businesspeople, and psychologists. A practitioner's group in the United States feels that the necessary background can include leadership positions, multicultural experience, teamwork, personal and organizational development, and knowledge of organizational learning (Turner, Lotz, & Cederholm, 1993). In a study of learning coaches, O'Neil (1999) found that although their professional backgrounds vary, many learning coaches tell stories of how in their past they had practiced action learning before they even knew what action learning was.

Characteristics, Attitudes, and Skills of Coaches

The literature paints a picture of the learning coach as having certain personal characteristics. First among these are authenticity—a person who relates to others as being real and genuine, with qualities of openness and frankness (Casey, 1991; Pearce, 1991). In addition, coaches need to be perceptive and insightful, and exhibit sensitivity and empathy with those insights (Casey, 1991). Equally important is an overwhelming desire to see others learn (Casey, 1991) and the curiosity and patience to watch that learning occur through the action learning process (Marsick, 1990). A learning coach must be persistent in the pursuit of his or her own knowledge (Marsick, 1990) and be willing to learn from both the participants and the process (Sewerin, 1997). Finally, there is a need to have a willingness to examine oneself critically in order to be aware of one's motives in being a learning coach (Sewerin, 1997).

One characteristic that respondents in O'Neil's (1999) study stressed is the need for maturity. This maturity can come from age and experience, although those are not the only sources. What was agreed on was that for someone to be a learning coach, he or she needed to be able to separate his or her own needs and feelings from that of the group, put aside those needs, and focus on the needs of the group.

Apart from the personal characteristics of the learning coach there are certain skill sets that are considered to be a prerequisite to becoming a learning coach.

Group Process Skills

One of the skill sets that a learning coach needs to develop is that of a process consultant (Casey, 1991; McGill & Beaty, 1995; O'Neil, 1997; O'Neil & Marsick, 1994; Weinstein, 1995). Reddy (1994) defines the role of a process consultant as "reasoned and intentional interventions, into the ongoing events and dynamics of a group, with the purpose of helping that group effectively attain its agreed-upon objectives" (p. 8). Schein (1988) goes on to say that the relationship between a group and a process consultant plays itself out through interventions that are made from an ambiguous power base, in the midst of ongoing work. Through these interventions, the process consultant builds involvement and commitment, and gains acceptance for the importance of looking at the process.

Similar to process consultation, coaching action learning takes place in a group or team context. A learning coach's activities are reasoned and intentional, and are intended to help the group or team attain its agreed-on objective of learning through solving an actual problem. Interventions are made in the midst of ongoing work (O'Neil, 1997). Lawrence (1991) says that every one of the skills that a process consultant must employ can also be used by a learning coach.

Although process consultation skills are important in performing the learning coach role, the role is more than that of a process consultant. The primary purpose of the learning coach is to help the group learn. This is in contrast to the purpose of a process consultant, whose primary charge is generally facilitating a group's work on its task. One implication of this difference is that a process consultant often intervenes to keep a group out of process difficulty, while a learning coach seeks to help the group learn from its difficulties. Among other things, this affects the timing of interventions. One experienced learning coach described the difference between process consultation and the learning coach role as follows (O'Neil, 1999):

> So the process consultant does all of those things. But at the same time, I'm not simply interested in process for its own sake. I'm interested in enabling individuals to ask themselves what they want to do before we meet again, what is the emerged plan after the process. I'm not saying there must be action. We get to the point where we leave the presenter with a choice as to what to do.

Systems Thinking

Some coaches use systems theory to help frame their work, and view the group and the action learning program as systems. For example, one coach uses a triangle to represent parts of a system—in this case the group, the sponsor, and the learning coach—and demonstrates how the interaction among these three elements in action learning can mirror the pull on the participants among the various elements within the organizational system (O'Neil, 1999).

Included in this system view is some basic knowledge of the environment in which the learning coach practices. All learning coaches need to have an understanding of learning processes in individuals and groups or teams (Pedler, 1996). Those who practice action learning within business organizations also need an understanding of organizational learning processes, an ability to have a systems or big-picture view, and some breadth of business experience (Bennett, 1990; Inglis, 1994; Pedler, 1996).

Personal Competencies

It seems almost to go without saying that learning coaches need good personal competencies that enable them to be effective when working with an action learning group, among them, keen powers of observation (Sewerin, 1997); the ability to give help, advice, and assistance; the ability to question, support, and challenge; and the ability to facilitate team members in giving and receiving help and feedback from each other (Pedler, 1996). The training that learning coaches receive should include the development and verification of these skill sets and competencies.

One characteristic that experienced action learning practitioners all agree they did not want in a learning coach is someone who presents himself or herself as an expert. One person put it this way:

> If somebody came along to me and said, "I have a master's degree in training development, and I'm a really experienced process consultant. I've studied action learning. I've read all of Revans's books," that would start to worry me. How is this person going to relate to these programs?

Making Learning Interventions: The Work of the Learning Coach

The primary work that a learning coach does with a group is in the form of interventions. This work requires both skill and art. The first step is deciding when to intervene. The skill of appropriately timing interventions in an action learning program—when to stay out and when to intervene in the group—is critical for learning coaches (Sewerin, 1997). This decision is complicated by the general principle that the group should learn from its own mistakes and difficulties. Unlike process consultants who generally seek to enforce group norms that allow a group to be productive, learning coaches must let the group stumble, encounter difficulties, and then help them, when necessary, to learn from the experience. One experienced coach described this process as follows:

> Well, you're sitting in a group, and an issue comes up where you can see they're going off. And you think about intervening. And you don't because you shouldn't intervene too often, should you? And then another problem comes up where you think, "I really ought to intervene," and you don't. The third time a problem comes up where you think, "Perhaps I should intervene," you struggle,

and you still don't intervene. And you intervene the fourth time — something comes up where you think they need some guidance. And as a general rule that struck me as being a closer desirable to a general one [O'Neil, 1999].

The decision to make an intervention can be based on several factors: intuition, cues from the verbal and nonverbal interaction of participants, and being asked to intervene. The coach may also use a variety of models or concepts — among them the Kolb (1984) and the Honey-Mumford (Mumford, 1995) learning style models and action science (Argyris, Putnam, & Smith, 1990) — that help frame how the coach views what is going on in the group.

In the northeast utility initiative discussed in Chapter Two, each participant takes the Honey-Mumford Learning Style Inventory. Aided by the learning coach, each team then discusses the strengths and weaknesses within the team based on the outcome of the inventory. The learning coach helps the team to use the information to understand team interaction better, provide one another feedback on that interaction, and improve the interaction within the team. These models and others like them are used to help participants start to understand their thoughts and assumptions. Group models like Tuckman's (1965) stage model of team development — forming, norming, storming, and performing — are frequently used phases for helping groups to examine their behavior and process. For example, the storming stage is very important and the model helps participants to understand what it's about. Systems models provide ways of understanding the actions of individuals in the group and the system, and the action of the group within the system.

> I do use a lot of systems stuff. They're very concerned with boundaries and how you manage them because they see boundaries so there's a whole set of linkings there that I use all the time, both for my work with the little group and with the organization [O'Neil, 1999].

In addition to applying cognitive models to their work, many coaches find themselves depending on their inner feelings for cues about when they might need to intervene. These coaches see themselves as instruments — that their inner feelings and self are pretty much all they have. This suggests the importance of learning coaches' having a capacity for giving a high level of attention to the quality of their focus on what is happening around them.

Intervention Methods and Practices

Many of the interventions that learning coaches make are similar to process consultation. However, the work of coaches goes beyond process consultation to a deeper level. The kinds of interventions that appear to differentiate the learning coach role are shown in Table 3.1, which also indicates the schools in which the intervention would most likely be used. Some of these interventions are discussed further below.

▲ **Table 3.1 Action Learning Interventions Related to Schools of Practice**

Action Learning Interventions	Action Learning Schools
Contracting • Continually changing and evolving • Emphasis on confidentiality	Scientific, experiential, critical reflection
Questioning • Favored approach for interventions • Ask naive questions to help participants to think in new ways; test beliefs and assumptions • Supportive, challenging, reflective, problem solving	Scientific, experiential, critical reflection
Reflection • Integral part of intervention work • Done at specific set times • Used when group is stuck or heading for difficulty • Often prompted by questions	Scientific, experiential, critical reflection
Critical reflection to help group • Work at different levels • Attribute different meanings to their thoughts and actions • Foster critical reflection on organization norms	Critical reflection

Programmed knowledge and just-in-time learning—share role of expert with group members	Experiential, critical reflection
Work with individual within the group setting	Scientific, experiential, critical reflection
Work with group to develop shared control of group process and learning process	Experiential, critical reflection
Help the group deal with the action learning process	Scientific, experiential, critical reflection
Help participants to give and receive help and feedback to each other	Experiential, critical reflection
Help the group deal with emotions generated by learning and task work	Experiential, critical reflection
Balance between task work and learning	
Make work visible	Experiential, critical reflection
Enable participants to develop their own hypotheses and assess alternatives	Scientific, experiential, critical reflection
Help design experiments	Scientific, experiential, critical reflection
Transfer of learning	Experiential, critical reflection
Enable learning • Create a support environment • Help rather than teach • Create ways to help think differently	Scientific, experiential, critical reflection
Challenge the group	Experiential, critical reflection
Say nothing and be invisible • Hold back on the intervention • Do nothing: just be there	Scientific, experiential, critical reflection
Transfer of learning coach skills	Scientific, experiential, critical reflection

Questioning

Most learning coaches would agree with the following statement: "It's all questions really, isn't it? It's all asking questions." No matter what the cause or intent of the intervention, most learning coaches use questions to help participants learn. Intervening with questions helps coaches to avoid slipping into a telling role (Bourner & Weinstein, 1996; Casey, 1991; Harrison & Miller, 1993; Marsick, 1990; Pearce, 1991; Pedler, 1991; Weinstein, 1995). The following quote from a coach highlights questioning:

> I think I asked the guy after he'd gone through a long process of analysis of his current situation, which was extremely threatening and seemed to be taking a single line, I said something like, "Have you thought of the involvement of venture capital in that?" I was opening up a field of thinking which he hadn't gone to at all. But it opened up the question for him into other ways. I don't have prescriptive questions that come out of a thing, but it might be something like, "Did you really understand what he was saying then, or is there more to it?" So it's kind of a little bit more challenging as opposed to supportive perhaps [O'Neil, 1999].

Reflection and Critical Reflection

As important as the questioning process is the reflection process (Garatt, 1984; Harrison, Miller, & Gibson, 1993; Inglis, 1994; Marsick, 1990; McGill & Beaty, 1995; O'Neil & Marsick, 1994; Weinstein, 1995). Depending on the school of action learning they may espouse, learning coaches undertake their reflection intervention differently. For those in the experiential school, reflection represents a cycle of reflection, action, and reflection on action, as well as reflection on the workings of the group (Garatt, 1984; McGill & Beaty, 1995). In some cases, reflection is scheduled at certain times during the group meeting, and at other times, the learning coach intervenes by asking the group to stop their activity to reflect on what has just happened.

For coaches more in the critical reflection school, the reflection may evolve to critical self-reflection on assumptions and critical reflection on the organization and its norms. The coach may be helping the participants work at more than one level or attribute different meanings to their thoughts and actions, as this coach said: "I learn from not just reflecting, but reflecting upon my process of reflecting, which is reflexive." One coach describes the process:

And then also to ask the difficult questions, and to go beyond the immediate symptom and to understand what really is going on for that person and get beyond that until something actually occurs which is an insight into the issue because they're able to see beyond the immediate answer that looks right from the textbook or from the box or from whatever [O'Neil, 1999].

Balance Between Task and Learning

The balance between task and learning is an integral part of action learning. Although the focus of the learning coach is on learning, an important part of that learning takes place through work on the task. As a result, learning coaches make interventions to help the group design experiments for gathering information about the problem and trying out different solutions, help with problem-solving strategies, and challenge participants to act when they would rather talk (Marsick, 1990).

Enabling Learning

Enabling learning is the primary role of the learning coach. Garratt (1984) describes the learning coach as a learning catalyst. This focus on learning starts early in the life of the group, since in the beginning a group is more inclined to focus on task, which drives out the learning (Lawrence, 1991; Weinstein, 1995). But as with other interventions, the learning coach works toward sharing power over the learning process (McGill & Beaty, 1995). The question, "So what have you learned from that?" is asked over and over until it becomes second nature for the participants to ask themselves and each other the same question (Weinstein, 1995, p. 177). This question helps participants to think about their work and work processes differently and to learn from them.

Coaches need to create an environment in which participants feel valued and secure. This encompasses being supportive and maintaining confidentially about what happens in the group or set.

Challenging the Group

Once a supportive environment has been established, the learning coach needs to decide how, and how far, to push a participant or the group as a whole to enable them to learn. One author asks, "Is a gentle and understanding approach the most beneficial? Or will the learning be greater through harsher confrontation?" (Weinstein, 1995, p. 207). Although many coaches feel that challenging is not the preferred choice of intervention, they believe that there are situations in which it is necessary, and sometimes it has a great impact:

> I mean, you have to struggle sometimes with somebody who is dominant, and you use a variety of methods for that which in other circumstances you may feel are not appropriate as a kind of personal challenge at some point or doing it for the group perhaps because it's impossible for them to do it in some circumstance. And I would say that's normally taboo, but in some circumstances it may be absolutely necessary and might even break the group, and maybe that's what's going to happen anyway [O'Neil, 1999].

Saying Nothing and Being Invisible

The principle of "saying nothing and being invisible" (Casey, 1991) manifests itself in a number of ways. It involves holding back and helping the group to grow by letting the members learn from their own mistakes and produce their own good answers (Marsick, 1990). This principle is practiced when a learning coach makes an explicit decision not to intervene in order to see if the group is able to respond to a participant who is acting aggressively (Weinstein, 1995). It is not stealing learning opportunities from the group. As one coach put it, "You need to get used to the fact that they're going to complain, `Well, why didn't you say that three hours ago?'"

Transfer of Learning Coach Skills

To work oneself out of a job through transferring the skills that the learning coach possesses to the group, so that the group can go on without him or her, is the ideal aim of the learning coach. This is accomplished through modeling the skills so that participants can learn to use them in the group and back at the workplace. Gradually the learning coach intervenes less and less. As one learning coach describes it, "What I do is support them to take over learning practices. After a while I don't have to do it. I just have to say one thing, and someone else tells what they see and then the others say what they see" (O'Neil, 1999).

Internal or External Learning Coaches?

Whether to use internal resources (within a company) or external resources (external consultants, academics) to perform the learning coach role is one of the choices that confront organizations. Unless experienced coaches are already members of the organization, initially there will be a dependence on external resources to develop an internal capability. Long term, there are both advantages and disadvantages to each choice. Table 3.2 summarizes the options.

Internal Coaches

An organization may have readily available people within the human resource organization who have some of the prerequisite skills for being a learning coach. If that is the case, they are already on the payroll and could be dedicated to the action learning initiative. By having these existing resources learn and play the role of learning coach, the skills will be readily available for transference to others in the organization.

One of the most important interventions in action learning is that of asking naive, fresh questions. The fact of being within the culture creates difficulty for the internal resource with this intervention. The learning

▲ **Table 3.2 Using Internal and External Learning Coaches: A Summary**

	Advantages	*Disadvantages*
Internal coaches	Readily available Less cost Ease in embedding skills within organization	Difficulty in operating outside the culture Difficulty in confronting participants within own culture Not readily available
External coaches	Experience Outsider to the culture	More cost More difficult to embed learning skills within organization

coach needs to challenge the group by putting a spotlight on taken-for-granted norms of behavior and thinking (Marsick, 1990). In addition to the difficulty in even recognizing these norms of behavior within yourself and others, the internal coach may need to confront others within the organization in ways that may cause the participant to react negatively to the coach. Finally, not all organizations have readily available resources. Cutbacks in human resources and line departments may make this option not possible.

External Coaches

There are a number of experienced practitioners of action learning available to help organizations think through whether action learning is the right intervention; if so, what school and design would best fit the needs; and help with the implementation of an initiative, including the learning coach role. Outside learning coaches do not encounter the same problems as those from inside the culture. They automatically operate outside the culture and do not run the same risks in challenging participants as someone who must return to work with them the next day. Yorks et al. (1996) saw the external learning coaches in the initiative as "sophisticated barbarians" (from Schön, 1987)—ones "who by their very nature as an outsider, are intended to see the situation through fresh eyes and then use those insights to raise critical questions to help reframe participants' understanding" (p. 318).

External coaches, however, cost money. Budgets, as well as people, are also at a premium in many organizations, so cost is a consideration in this decision. Finally, most action learning practitioners espouse the philosophy of transferring their skills to participants and the organization. So with external resources doing most, if not all, of the learning coach work, specific attention has to be paid to how these skills will become embedded in the organization.

Training New Learning Coaches

There is general agreement in the literature about the basics of developing new learning coaches (McGill & Beaty, 1992; Pedler, 1996; Weinstein, 1995). The first step is to have prospective coaches participate in an action learning program. Generally unless an individual experiences the process as a participant, it is difficult for him or her to understand and support participants in the future. This is not always easy to accomplish if the decision is made to use entirely internal resources. As a result, organizations may opt to use external resources to help start a program, moving as expeditiously as possible to internal resources. Attendance as a participant can then be followed up by the new learning coach's shadowing an experienced coach in a program, working with a group with an experienced coach as a mentor, or plunging right in to work with a group.

Research suggests that some content training may also be appropriate, depending on the background of a new coach (O'Neil, 1999). In order to develop a theoretical base for their work, new learning coaches need to understand the background for forming that base. This should involve an introduction to the different approaches to action learning and an examination of their assumptions about learning.

The fundamentals of the adult learning theories of learning from experience and transformative learning should be included as a part of learning coach development. Consistent with action learning theory, this content learning should be reflected on in the light of the new coach's experience as a participant in action learning.

If new learning coaches do not have group process skills as part of their repertoire, a formal class or developmental opportunity should be incorporated as part of their development. In any case, it is important that the new coach understand the differences between process consultation and the learning coach role.

Conclusion

This chapter has just begun to scratch the surface of the complex role of the learning coach. As we have already noted, we advocate the critical reflection school when it fits the needs of an organization, and the learning coach is a crucial part of that school. The coach enables a group to engage in the critical questioning and challenging that needs to happen for critical reflection and transformative learning to occur.

Action learning is a process that requires an investment of time, resources, and energy, and a learning coach can help to ensure that participants and the organization get as much as possible out of their investment.

References

Argyris, C., Putnam, R., & Smith, D. M. (1985). *Action science.* San Francisco: Jossey-Bass.

Bennett, R. (1990). Effective set advising in action learning programmes. *Journal of European Industrial Training, 14*(7), 28–30.

Bourner, T., & Weinstein, K. (1996). Just another talking shop? Some of the pitfalls in action learning. *Employee Counseling Today, 8*(6), 57–68.

Casey, D. (1991). The role of the set advisor. In M. Pedler (Ed.), *Action learning in practice* (2nd ed., pp. 261–273). Brookfield, VT: Gower.

Garratt, B. (1984). Don't call me teacher. In D. Casey & D. Pearce (Eds.), *More than management development: Action learning at GEC* (pp. 79–90). Hampshire, England: Gower.

Harries, J. M. (1991). Developing the set advisor. In M. Pedler (Ed.), *Action learning in practice* (2nd ed., pp. 275–284). Brookfield, VT: Gower.

Harrison, R., & Miller, S. (1993). Doctors in management: Two into one won't go—Or will it? Part I. *Executive Development 6*(2), 9–13.

Harrison, R., Miller, S., & Gibson, A. (1993). Doctors in management—Part II: Getting into action. *Executive Development 6*(4), 3–7.

Inglis, S. (1994). *Making the most of action learning.* Brookfield, VT: Gower.

Kolb, D. (1984). *Experiential learning.* Englewood Cliffs, NJ: Prentice Hall.

Lawlor, A. (1991). The components of action learning. In M. Pedler (Ed.), *Action learning in practice* (2nd ed., pp. 247–259). Brookfield, VT: Gower.

Lawrence, J. (1991). Action learning—A questioning approach. In A. Mumford (Ed.), *Gower handbook of management development* (3rd ed., pp. 214–247). Brookfield, VT: Gower.

Marsick, V. J. (1990). Action learning and reflection in the workplace. In J. Mezirow and Associates, *Fostering critical reflection in adulthood* (pp. 23–46). San Francisco: Jossey-Bass.

Marsick, V. J., & Watkins, K. E. (1992). *Informal and incidental learning in the workplace.* London: Routledge.

McGill, I., & Beaty, L. (1992). *Action learning: A practitioner's guide.* London: Kogan Page.

Mumford, A. (1992). So what is the role of the set adviser? In K. Weinstein (Ed.), *Action Learning News, 11*(1), 14–15.

Mumford, A. (1995). *Learning at the top.* Berkshire, England: McGraw-Hill.

O'Neil, J. (1997). Set advising: More than just process consultancy? In M. Pedler (Ed.), *Action learning in practice* (3rd ed., pp. 243–256). London: Gower.

O'Neil, J. A. (1999). *The role of the learning adviser in action learning.* Unpublished dissertation. Teachers College, Columbia University, New York.

O'Neil, J., & Marsick, V. J. (1994). Becoming critically reflective through action reflection learning. In A. Brooks & K. Watkins (Eds.), *The emerging power of action inquiry technologies* (pp. 17–30). New Directions for Adult and Continuing Education, no. 63. San Francisco: Jossey-Bass.

O'Neil, J., Marsick, V. J., Yorks, L., Nilson, G., & Kolodny, R. (1997). Life on the seesaw: Tensions in action reflection learning. In M. Pedler (Ed.), *Action learning in practice* (3rd ed., pp. 339–346). London: Gower.

Pearce, D. (1991). Appendix 1: Getting started: An action learning manual. In M. Pedler (Ed.), *Action learning in practice* (2nd ed., pp. 349–366). Brookfield, VT: Gower.

Pedler, M. (1991). Questioning ourselves. In M. Pedler (Ed.), *Action learning in practice* (2nd ed., pp. 63–70). Brookfield, VT: Gower.

Pedler, M. (1996). *Action learning for managers.* London: Lemos & Crane.

Reddy, W. B. (1994). *Intervention skills: Process consultation for small groups and teams.* San Diego, CA: Pfeiffer.

Revans, R. W. (1978). *The a. b. c. of action learning: A review of 25 years of experience.* Salford, England: University of Salford.

Revans, R. W. (1991). Action learning: Its origins and nature. In M. Pedler (Ed.), *Action learning in practice* (2nd ed., pp. 3–16). Brookfield, VT: Gower.

Schein, E. H. (1988). *Process consultation.* Reading, MA: Addison-Wesley.

Schön, D. A. (1987). *Educating the reflective practitioner.* San Francisco: Jossey-Bass.

Sewerin, T. (1997, April). The MiL learning coach. In *MiL Concepts.* Lund, Sweden: MiL Institute.

Tuckman, B. W. (1965). Developmental sequence in small groups. *Psychological Bulletin, 65,* 384–399.

Turner, E., Lotz, S., & Cederholm, L. (1993). *The ARL project team advisor's handbook.* New York: Leadership in International Management.

Weinstein, K. (1995). *Action learning: A journey in discovery and development.* London: HarperCollins.

Yorks, L., O'Neil, J., Marsick, V. J., Nilson, G. E., & Kolodny, R. (1996). Boundary management in action reflection learning research: Taking the role of a sophisticated barbarian. *Human Resource Development Quarterly, 7*(4), 313–329.

Chapter 4

Transfer of Learning from Action Learning Programs to the Organizational Setting

Lyle Yorks
Sharon Lamm
Judy O'Neil

The Problem and the Solution. Many times learning never finds its way to actual practices in organizations. There are predictable barriers to the transfer of learning. This chapter examines the factors that both facilitate and inhibit learning transfer to the organizational setting and provides practical guidance.

Facilitating the transfer of learning from training and development programs to the workplace setting has long been the Achilles' heel of human resource development. Estimates of wasted training dollars run into the billions of dollars. Transfer is especially problematic in management training in which there is "tremendous leeway in what a manager or supervisor needs to know and the contexts in which he or she might apply that knowledge" (Laker, 1990, p. 219). This need for generalizability of transfer has been conceptualized in terms of distance and called *far transfer* (Butterfield & Nelson, 1989; Laker, 1990; Royer, 1979). Far transfer requires more than the establishment of a repertoire of behaviors; it requires the ability to think and take action in diverse, complex, and uncertain contexts.

The theory and rhetoric of action learning assert that these kinds of programs produce significant learning and that the design of these programs should enhance transfer, since a certain degree of transfer is built into the program design. A growing body of empirical evidence demonstrates the kind of learning that occurs in action learning programs

(Lamm, forthcoming; Willis, Deans, & Jones, 1998; Yorks et al., 1998). Less is known about the outcomes of this learning beyond the action learning experience itself (Willis et al., 1998). This is essentially a learning transfer question and involves considerations such as initiation of subsequent actions based on what was experienced in the program and the maintenance, or continuing application, of what was learned overtime. We need to know more about how the action learning experience is carried forward into other arenas of a participant's life. For example, Lamm (forthcoming) found that many participants in an action learning program in a global automotive company applied their learning to work and home life (for example, self-discovery led to humility and balance in the workplace and personal life).

This chapter examines the question of learning transfer from action learning programs and suggests ways of enhancing transfer to the workplace. We begin with a brief discussion of what is meant by transfer of learning and the kind of learning desired from these programs. Next we examine the literature on training transfer and, based on our own experience and research, make specific recommendations. Our discussion focuses on two areas: program design and organizational climate for learning transfer. The context of our discussion is on action learning programs implemented in organizations with the intention of developing the managerial competencies while addressing critical strategic issues.

Conceptualizing the Transfer of Learning

Broadly defined, the extent to which transfer of learning occurs depends on the degree to which changes in knowledge, insight, understanding, meaning, attitudes, competencies, or behaviors are applied by the learner outside the program. When the action learning program is sponsored by an employer, the desired transfer is to the workplace. This point is not trivial since a learner may gain new insights and competencies but conclude that applying them on the job would be futile. A manager from Singapore told us during an interview, "You shouldn't judge how much I learned from what I do later. I have changed a lot inside in how I view things. It may not show in how I choose to act at work." In this situation, attitudes may have changed, but learning transfer, at least in terms of behavior at work, did not happen.

The intent of action learning is to generate what Revans calls Q learning, or questioning insight. This is especially important for helping managers to function effectively in rapidly changing, complex task environments and to develop competencies for responding to diverse and novel situations (Marsick & Cederholm, 1988). At a minimum, Q learning implies what Cell (1984) calls situation learning—a change in how one interprets a situation, through altering either one's values or judgment of how things work in a particular situation. This is similar to Mezirow's discussion of learning new meaning schemes, Argyris and Schön's description of double-loop learning (1974), and Bateson's (1972) concept of Level II learning—changing the set of alternatives from which one selects actions. Transfer can be said to occur when a person effectively acts on this altered judgment of the situation.

All action learning programs strive for transfer of this type around the task and hope for it to occur around certain managerial competencies as well. Many programs, especially those using critical reflection, seek to develop what Cell calls transsituation learning: learning how to change one's interpretations of situations through interpreting one's acts of interpretation (what many writers, including Cell, refer to as learning to learn). Here transfer of learning would involve ongoing practice of reflection and critical reflection when confronted with problematic or novel situations.

Another type of learning, which does not fall comfortably into Cell's model, is Mezirow's concept of perspective transformation: "becoming aware, through reflection and critique, of specific presuppositions upon which a distorted or incomplete meaning perspective is based and then transforming that perspective through a reorganization of meaning" (1991, p. 94). This change in interpretive framework is more comprehensive than a single-meaning scheme and changes not only how one views a certain situation, but results in reinterpreting a wide range of situations in one's past. In a very real sense, the learning is developmental and emancipatory in nature. It is the same as Bateson's Level III learning—changes in the premises on which our perspective, or assumptive frame of reference, are based.

Our point is that the learning that is sought from action learning programs is different from straightforward instrumental (Mezirow, 1991) or response learning (Bateson, 1972; Cell, 1984)—the kind of learning that has been the focus on much of the literature on training transfer. Studies of this kind of learning have focused on the transfer of fairly specific skills, such as computer skills (Kontoghiorghes, 1998), procedural legal aspects for desk clerks in a bank (Gielen, 1996), time management practices (Wexley & Baldwin, 1986), safety rule training (Reber & Wallen, 1984), brainstorming and brainwriting for problem solving (Gist, 1989), and specific negotiation techniques such as controlled enthusiasm, direct appeals to an opponent's interests, and a "broken record" approach to unyielding opponents (Gist, Bavetta, & Stevens, 1990). The transfer that occurs with this kind of learning is generally of the kind that Salomon and Perkins (1989) call *low road transfer* and *forward-reaching high road transfer*. Low road transfer involves the straightforward application of behaviors learned in one context to another with little modification. This is in contrast to high road transfer, in which the learner applies an explicitly known general principle to a new situation. In forward-reaching high road transfer, "the principle is so well learned . . . as a general principle that it simply suggests itself appropriately on later occasions" (p. 119).

In action learning programs the kind of transfer that is sought is closer to Salomon's and Perkins's concept of backward-reaching high road transfer, involving the explicit conscious formulation of abstraction of the new situation to guide a reaching back to experience for relevant connections. Backward-reaching transfer occurs when a person confronting a unique or new situation conceptualizes key characteristics of the situation and, based on this conceptualization, extrapolates a course of action from previous experience or training. This kind of transfer is especially sought in the case of action learning programs that place a strong emphasis on reflection or critical reflection. In these programs the reflective behavior generic to backward-reaching transfer is part of what is intended to be developed through the action learning experience. Backward-reaching high road transfer can also occur in instrumental learning, such as when someone encounters a new screen on his or her computer and through reflection on previous training determines the correct way to manipulate the options presented. In interpersonal competencies such as negotiation skills, this kind of transfer can be said to occur when a person reflects on previous training and seeks to apply the skill learned in the current situation. The differentiating characteristic of backward-reaching high road transfer is that it involves an element of conceptual reflection.

There is a long history of conceptual development and research on the influence of program design on training transfer. Recently increasing attention has been given to the role played by organizational climate for transfer. Below we look at the connection among concepts of training design, action learning, and transfer and make some recommendations regarding the practice of action learning. Next we look at the pattern of transfer obtained from action learning programs in corporate contexts and assess this experience from the perspective of transfer climate. Additional recommendations for learning transfer are made.

Program Design from a Transfer-of-Learning Perspective

Something of a symbiotic relationship exists between the design of action learning programs and the notion of transfer. In terms of their design philosophy, action learning programs involve the direct transfer of questioning insight around the task or problem through the cycles of action and reflection on the project. Team meetings also provide subcycles of action and reflection as participants reflect on their behaviors in the group's process, challenge one another's assumptions about their thinking around the task, and discuss how they might work together more effectively. In action learning programs in which participants have individual problems, these same cycles of action and reflection enable participants to challenge and be challenged about their individual problems.

The issue of learning transfer is complicated by the notion of what kind of learning one is expecting to transfer. As noted above, learning and acting on new meaning schemes around the project or problem are basic to the design. Experts note that there is a difference between programs that culminate with recommendations to sponsors of projects and those that focus on having participants involved in the implementation of recommendations. Administrators of action learning programs that emphasize participant involvement in the consequences of their actions suggest that learning around the task is reinforced through continuing workplace application. This becomes particularly true in designs that call for work on individual problems.

In the case of perspective transformation, the notion of transfer is in one sense irrelevant. A person with an enhanced meaning perspective will, by definition, view his or her subsequent experiences differently. This new perspective is likely to influence their behavior in ways too numerous to measure in any traditional sense of the term. Indeed, a changed meaning perspective may lead to changes not anticipated by an organization, such as striving for a new balance in one's life or even leaving the organization. Others may choose not to act on new insights in the organizational setting, as the manager from Singapore suggested.

Our focus here is on learning transfer to the workplace in ways that are aligned with the general intentions of the organization. In the next section we consider some basic concepts and principles of program design from the literature on training transfer. This literature focuses more on skill transfer from instrumental learning. The objectives of many action learning programs are to develop new meaning schemes around the organization's strategic focus and alignment, and develop competencies that are supportive of that focus. Generally action learning has been used to develop organizational competencies that are consistent with significant reorientation of the organization's direction, such as going global and requiring new behaviors (for example, participatory teamwork that may involve working laterally across traditional lines of hierarchy or influence; Dennis, Cederholm, & Yorks, 1997; Dixon, 1998).

We believe, however, that the general thrust of this literature can provide insight into enhancing learning transfer by guiding how learning coaches seek to maximize the potential of the interaction between Revans's P and Q learning.

Some Basic Concepts of Training Transfer

From a learning design perspective, action learning programs should facilitate learning transfer because they are consistent with concepts that have long standing in the transfer of training literature. For example, when learning coaches encourage participants to identify and reflect on the variation of experience in applying certain management competencies or action around the task, this can be seen as practicing McGehee and Thayer's (1961) general principle concept. The general principle asserts that learning transfer is facilitated when the principles that underlie the training content are taught. A distinction between how this principle has been traditionally used in training and its application in action learning is found in the timing and mode of delivery of content, or P training. In programs that include just-in-time learning, principles are highlighted that are linked to the learning needs emerging during the program. This links the general principle with another long-held training concept, the most teachable moment (Havighurst, 1961).

If subsequent reflection periods continue to raise the consciousness of participants to these principles and how they apply in different contexts, the effect is similar to Ellis's (1965) concept of stimulus variability. This concept holds that positive transfer is enhanced when a variety of stimuli are employed. Further, the design of action learning programs includes issues directly relevant to the workplace and spaces meetings over time. This provides for distributed practice, another principle long promulgated in the training literature (Briggs & Naylor, 1962). This distribution of practice, with the added caveat that central to the program design is the assumption that learners will encounter difficulties in taking action on challenging and complex issues, allows for these difficulties to be examined in the context of the learning environment.

Recent research has examined goal setting and behavior self-management as methods for enhancing behavioral change following management training programs. Wexley and Baldwin (1986), in their study of participants in a time management training program, found goal setting to be superior to behavior self-management in inducing behavioral change over a two-month period following the training. Gist et al. (1990) found a more differentiated effect in their study of the transfer of negotiation skills to novel tasks. In their study, goal-setting trainees use skills more repeatedly than behavioral self-management trainees do in novel task situations. Self-management trainees had a higher rate of skill generalization and higher overall performance levels on the transfer task. Elements of both strategies have relevance for action learning programs. Learning coaches can work with participants to identify learning goals prior to the start of an action learning program, a practice already followed in some action learning programs. Participants can be encouraged to reflect on these goals throughout the program and set subsequent goals for continuation of learning following the program. At the same time they can develop strategies for self-management around anticipated obstacles, based on their experience during the program. In programs in which participants work on individual projects, a kind of goal setting happens each time the participant plans action in connection with his or her project, so this method of transfer is actually an inherent part of the design.

Linking performance goals to knowledge of results or feedback has also been demonstrated to be effective for facilitating transfer in safety training (Komaki, Heinzmann, & Lawson, 1980; Reber & Wallin, 1984). This linkage also has application in action learning programs through the cycle of action and reflection. Each time a participant or participants take action in connection with their project, the organization provides real-time feedback that can be taken back to the action learning team and examined through reflection and additional questioning. Other programs use personal development activities that include feedback linked to learning from the program.

Implications for Design

Based on the literature discussed above, we believe the following program design practices become salient. These practices place emphasis on the design features already part of many action learning programs, especially those in the scientific, experiential, and critical reflection schools.

- Linking the general principle with the concept of the most teachable moment, P learning around competencies should be available at the time participants are encountering difficulty and express this difficulty during reflection periods. This learning could be supplied by the learning coach, a knowledgeable participant, or an outside resource. For example, effective team practices should be discussed when it becomes evident that a project team is experiencing difficulties. An explicit link can then be made between the principle and the group's experience. This suggests that most time in action learning programs should be spent in project work, with content learning spaced throughout. Different teams may receive different content inputs.

- Linkages between general principles and stimulus variability can be made through reflection within the teams and among teams with programs designed with several teams. During periods of reflection, learning coaches increasingly can draw attention to how current issues in the group are similar in principle to those experienced earlier. Dialogues among teams can be structured so that experiences are shared, with learning coaches encouraging reflection on points where similar principles and practices have been useful in different contexts.

- Programs that space meetings across time allow participants to try out new behaviors back on the job. Learning coaches can encourage participants to reflect on actions taken back in the workplace and discuss these at the next program day. This should be more effective from a learning perspective than programs conducted in highly compressed time frames.

- Learning coaches can work with participants to set learning goals prior to the start of the program. These goals can periodically be the focus of individual reflection throughout the program. A company that was conducting an action learning program in which four one-week residential meetings were scheduled over a five-month period had participants form learning support groups. The only guideline was that membership in the support group should be separate from one's project team. These groups of two to four participants met periodically each program week to discuss their personal learning goals in terms of their experiences in the program. Ideally these support groups can function as action learning sets, providing for action learning within the action learning program.
- Reflection and dialogue sessions within project teams or learning support groups can be focused on anticipated obstacles to transferring learning to the organization. These obstacles can be both organizational and personal in nature, and the reflection can be around developing self-maintenance plans.
- Action learning programs can have a built-in developmental feedback component, such as a 360-degree feedback process. This feedback should be of benefit to each participant. On a voluntary basis, participants can discuss the feedback with learning coaches or project team members during the program. Another round of feedback can be provided at some point following the program.

Patterns of Learning Transfer: Observations from the Field

Following are descriptions of learning transfer from two organizations. Table 4.1 provides a summary of how each program incorporated the practices discussed above.

A comprehensive field study in an organization using action learning to transform itself from a multinational to a truly global organization reveals some interesting patterns of learning transfer (Yorks et al., 1998). First, there was learning from the projects. These projects involved issues in the development of globally integrated structures, systems, and practices such as logistics, financial statements, and organizational structures. Learning from working on these projects clearly transferred to other areas of the managers' lives. There were repeated instances of self-initiated actions across organizational lines that never would have happened

Table 4.1 Transfer Design Practices as Applied in Two Corporate Action Learning Programs

Design Practice	Food Products Company	Public Utility
Link general principle with teachable moment	Moderate application: Program weeks heavily focused on communitywide learning, P learning linked to general needs; learning coaches provide just-in-time learning	Team project, moderate application: P learning linked to general program needs, learning coaches provided just-in-time learning in teams Individual learning goal project, strong application: Cycle of reflection and action on goal with questioning by coach and other participants
Link general principles with stimulus variability	Strong application: Learning coaches make links in frequent reflection periods	Team project and individual learning goal project, strong application: Learning coaches make links in frequent reflection periods
Distributed application	Moderate to strong application: Program involved four six-day weeks of formal meeting time spread over four months; community dialogue about workplace application encouraged, especially toward end of program	Team project and individual learning goal project, moderate application: Program involves six half-days with the coach, spread over a six-week period; teams meet without the learning coach in between formal meetings

(Continued)

▲ **Table 4.1   Continued**

Design Practice	Food Products Company	Public Utility
Learning goals	Moderate application: Participants encouraged to set learning goals in private support groups; learning coaches provided coaching around goals when asked by participant	Strong application: Each participant develops learning goals with coach and shares them with the team; frequent periods of reflection and questioning around these goals throughout program
Self-maintenance plans	Not done	Not done
Developmental feedback	Strong application: 360-degree feedback provided during and following the program	Individual learning goal project, moderate application: Model of feedback provided to participants with the expectation that they provide feed back to each other throughout the program; coach also provides feedback

before the implementation of the program. These ongoing actions continued for well over a year following the program. In addition, the development of this global perspective was credited by the executive team for facilitating the change to a global organizational structure.

Transfer around competencies, which the program also sought to develop, was more differentiated. About 80 percent of the people interviewed reported seeing changes in managers who participated in the program. The most frequently mentioned changes were the sharing of information with subordinates and peers, listening and an openness to the opinions of others, a higher level of reflection, and encouragement of dialogue.

However, these changes were not universal. When asked about the proportion of people changing, estimates ranged from half to three-quarters of those attending. Also there was a pattern of some relapse or slippage in behavior. These reports of relapse were coupled with reports of the new behavior being retriggered by events. For example, one respondent described a meeting with a group of managers that included two who had attended the action learning program. They were essentially dominating the discussion and arguing. He asked if this behavior was what they were learning in the action learning program. They both acknowledged that it was not and changed their behavior. The respondent went on to describe a very productive meeting.

The overall pattern in this organization was that transfer of these behaviors was most visible when senior managers were vocal in their support of the competencies and strove to model them, no matter how imperfectly; managers felt supported in their efforts to transfer them; and the nature of one's job supported application of new learning. This support might come from more senior managers or colleagues. A theme that emerged from the interviews was that the program had created a capacity for new behavior, but this capacity needed to be triggered by events in the environment.

This program was characterized by a good amount of transfer. Reference to Table 4.1 demonstrates that all but one of the transfer principles were contained in the program's design. Still, opportunities to enhance the potential for transfer further clearly existed. (The sustained transfer of learning from this program led to a change in the organization's culture, a topic covered in Chapter Six.)

A large northeastern utility is using action learning to help transform itself from a regulated, hierarchical company to one that can be successful in an unregulated environment. The action learning program is primarily focused on supervisors and has set out the following objectives in order to help bring about the transformation.

- Enhancing the way people communicate, interact, and work together
- Weaving quality management tools and behaviors into the fabric of the organization
- Developing and using problem-solving and coaching skills
- Building an environment of openness and trust and surfacing and resolving conflict

The utility evaluates the impact of the program primarily through telephone calls to participants on a schedule of one month, two months, and after completion of the program. Each call explores critical incidents that the participant has dealt with during the period. It is through these calls that we are able to gather information on the level of learning transfer.

In this program, each team has a project, and each participant establishes one or more personal learning goals, which become essentially individual projects over the course of the program. Evaluation results demonstrate that both learning from team projects and individual learning goals are being transferred into the organization. For example, the following comment reflects learning around quality tools and behaviors: "Any time that we have process or procedure problems, we go through the seven-step process. People are actually doing it." Another participant described changes in his skill in building interpersonal relationships. He attributed the changes in his attitude toward his dealings with regulators from another state to the program, stating: "I am quite sure that I would not have set up a follow-up meeting with these people if this had happened prior to the program."

As in the global food company action learning project, these changes are not universal, but they are at a fairly high percentage. Organizationwide evaluation results show that depending on the learning objective, 65 percent to 79 percent of former participants are seeing changes in the organization. Those who report little or no change most often attribute this lack of transfer to the entrenched culture of their part of the company or doubts about the support of upper management for the changes.

Transfer Climate

The literature on training transfer has also focused on the work environment as another factor influencing transfer (Baldwin & Ford, 1988; Tannenbaum & Yukl, 1992). The concept of transfer climate has been advanced as a mediating variable between the organizational setting and an individual's motivation to change behavior on the job. Transfer climate is seen as either supporting or inhibiting the application of learning to the job (Mathieu, Tannenbaum, & Salas, 1992; Rouiller & Goldstein, 1993). Rouiller and Goldstein suggest that transfer climate may be as important as the design of the training program in explaining transfer of learning. Recently Holton and Bates and their colleagues (Bates, Holton, & Seyler, 1997; Holton, Bates, Seyler, & Carvalho, 1997; Holton, Bates, Ruona, & Leimbach, 1998) have developed a generalized learning transfer climate questionnaire (LTQ), which provides a basis for measuring climate and provides construct validation. As is the case with the broader literature on training transfer, the primary focus of the transfer climate literature is on behavioral skill training delivered in a classroom format. However, the variables included in the LTQ have relevance for action learning, especially in the light of the patterns of transfer described above.

We will limit our discussion here to four factors generally considered to be important to transfer climate: peer support, management support, perceived content validity, and motivational components in terms of the personal outcomes experienced by participants who transfer skills and competencies to the workplace. Our discussion treats these factors as qualitative categories, as opposed to the quantitative variables in instruments such as the LTQ.

Both management and peer support seem critical in the decision of participants to apply learning back in the workplace. Management support is demonstrated in various ways, including sponsoring projects for the program and modeling the learning process back in the workplace. Peer support is also important, as the following comment from an interview in the multinational food company illustrates: "In the beginning, it was very difficult to say 'Let's have some reflection.' Others would say, 'Let him have his fun,' then go on with the meeting. Now the number of people who know reflection is growing."

In addition to management and peer support, support can come from subordinates, as illustrated in following comment by a manager about one of his unit supervisors who came back from another action learning program: "One of my people came back from an action learning workshop, and I saw him using the skills with me. This was helpful; I felt supported."

Validity of learning content takes two forms in action learning programs. The first is whether there is a compelling business reason for the program, which justifies the cost as well as the time and energy demanded of participants. The second is whether there is acknowledgment in the organization that this compelling business reason demands new learning around both tasks and competencies.

For example, in the multinational food company, the action learning program was preceded by several events. First, management repeatedly made the case that it was necessary for the company to transform itself into a global organization in order to align itself better to its customer base. Second, this message was validated through a search conference that produced a global vision. (A search conference is a large system change intervention where a significant number of people are brought together in order to surface and build consensus around issues of organizational direction such as vision, mission, and strategies.) Yet participants in this conference also expressed doubt about the organization's ability to make such a transformation. Both management's articulation of the need for a globalization strategy and the search conference contributed to the compelling need for the program. Establishing the global network became the theme of the program.

Third, following the search conference, an organizational culture survey documented skepticism throughout the organization about senior management's commitment to globalization, validated the strategic concept, and documented gaps in specific competencies between what existed and what would be required in a global organization. This survey provided validation for the program content (much of the P learning in the program was linked to survey outcomes) and reinforced the need for the program. These events set the stage for the action learning program and were repeatedly cited by the program coordinator. Most of the participants in the action learning program had been involved in the search conference and the culture survey.

Another important part of the transfer climate is the personal outcomes of those seeking to apply the practices learned in the program (Holton et al., 1997). If these outcomes are positive in terms of performance, rewards, and career opportunities, the climate favors transfer. If such personal outcomes are negative, the opposite is true. In the case of this program, our data do not allow us to address the longer-term outcomes. However, early evidence showed that those former participants who were continuing to demonstrate learning from the program back on the job were being chosen for new assignments and opportunities in the company as the globalization strategy began to be implemented in the form of a new organizational structure and new assignments.

Certain questions relative to transfer climate suggest themselves to be asked by any human resource development specialist considering initiating an action learning intervention:

- Does the organization face a compelling strategic challenge that has been well articulated in the organization?
- Are there compelling reasons for people to change how they relate to one another and develop new networks of relationships?
- Is there a documented desire within the organization to increase its capacity for learning?
- Are senior managers in the organization willing to change their own behaviors to model the way?
- Are senior managers willing to participate in the growth of people through providing feedback and engaging in dialogue?

The answers to these questions begin the process of assessing the transfer of learning climate. They should be part of a broader assessment process regarding organizational readiness for action learning (see Chapter Seven).

Conclusion

In this chapter we have explored the steps that human resource development specialists and learning coaches might take to facilitate the transfer of learning from action learning programs to the workplace. These recommendations are based on inference from the literature on training transfer and our action learning experience and research. They need to be explored further and validated through future experience and rigorous comparative field research, possibly using grounded theory methods. Application of these recommendations requires skillful, reflective practice on the part of learning coaches. If organizations are seeking effective transfer of learning to the workplace, explicit attention needs to be given to the dynamics of transfer in both program design and organizational context.

References

Argyris, C., & Schön, D. A. (1974). *Theory in practice: Increasing professional effectiveness.* San Francisco: Jossey-Bass.

Baldwin, T. T., & Ford, J. K. (1988). Transfer of training: A review and directions for future research. *Personnel Psychology, 41,* 63–105.

Bates, R. A., Holton, E. F. III, & Seyler, D. L. (1997). Factors affecting the transfer of training in an industrial setting. In R. Torracco (Ed.), *Academy of Human Resource Development Conference Proceedings.* Baton Rouge, LA: Academy of Human Resource Development.

Bateson, G. (1972). *Steps to an ecology of the mind.* New York: Ballantine Books.

Briggs, G. E., & Naylor, J. C. (1962). The relative efficiency of several training methods as a function of transfer task complexity. *Journal of Experimental Psychology, 56,* 492–500.

Butterfield, E. C., & Nelson, G. D. (1989). Theory and practice of teaching for transfer. *Educational Research and Development, 37*(4), 5–38.

Cell, E. (1984). *Learning to learn from experience.* Albany: State University of New York Press.

Dennis, C. B., Cederholm, L., & Yorks, L. (1996). Learning your way to a global organization. In K. Watkins & V. J. Marsick (Eds.), *In action: Creating the learning organization* (pp. 165–177). Alexandria, VA: American Society for Training and Development.

Dixon, N. (1998). Building global capacity with global task teams. *Performance Improvement Quarterly, 11*(1), 108–112.

Ellis, H. C. (1965). *The transfer of learning.* New York: McGraw-Hill.

Gielen, E. W. M. (1996). Transfer of training in a corporate setting: Testing a model. In E. Holton (Ed.), *Academy of Human Resource Development Conference Proceedings* (pp. 434–441). Baton Rouge, LA: Academy of Human Resource Development.

Gist, M. E. (1989). The influence of training method on self-efficacy and idea generation among managers. *Personnel Psychology, 42,* 787–805.

Gist, M. E., Bavetta, A. G., & Stevens, C. K. (1990). Transfer training method: Its influence on skill generation, skill repetition, and performance level. *Personnel Psychology, 43,* 501–523.

Havighurst, R. J. (1961). *Developmental tasks and education.* New York: David McKay Company.

Holton III, E. F., Bates, R. A., Ruona, W. E. A., & Lembach, M. (1998). Development and validation of a generalized learning transfer questionnaire: Final report. In R. J. Torraco (Ed.), *Academy of Human Resource Development Conference Proceedings* (pp. 482–489). Baton Rouge, LA: Academy of Human Resource Development.

Holton III, E. F., Bates, R. A., Seyler, D. L., & Carvalho, M. B. (1997). Toward construct validation of a transfer climate instrument. *Human Resource Development Quarterly, 8,* 91–113.

Komaki, J., Heinzmann, A. T., & Lawson, L. (1980). Effect of training and feedback: Component analysis of a behavioral safety program. *Journal of Applied Psychology, 65,* 261–270.

Kontoghiorghes, C. (1998). Training transfer as it relates to the instructional system and the broader work environment. In R. J. Torraco (Ed.), *Academy of Human Resource Development Conference Proceedings* (pp. 466–473). Baton Rouge, LA: Academy of Human Resource Development.

Laker, D. R. (1990). Dual dimensionality of training transfer. *Human Resource Development Quarterly, 1,* 209–223.

Lamm, S. (forthcoming). *Transformational learning and leadership in the context of action reflection learning: A case study in global organization.* Unpublished doctoral dissertation, Teachers College, Columbia University, New York.

Marsick, V. J., & Cederholm, L. (1988). Developing leadership in international managers—An urgent challenge. *Columbia Journal of World Business, 23*(4), 3–11.

Mathieu, J. E., Tannenbaum, S. I., & Salas, E. (1992). Influences of individual and situational characteristics on measures of training effectiveness. *Academy of Management Journal, 35,* 828–847.

McGehee, W., & Thayer, P. W. (1961). *Training in business and industry.* New York: Wiley.

Mezirow, J. (1991). *Transformative dimensions of adult learning.* San Francisco: Jossey-Bass.

Reber, R. A., & Wallin, J. A. (1984). The effects of training, goal setting, and knowledge of results on safe behavior: A component analysis. *Academy of Management Journal, 27,* 544–560.

Revans, R. W. (1978). *The a, b, c of action learning: A review of twenty-five years of experience.* Salford, England: University of Salford.

Rouiller, J. Z., & Goldstein, I. L. (1993). The relationship between organizational transfer climate and positive transfer of training. *Human Resource Development Quarterly, 4*, 377–390.

Royer, J. M. (1979). Theories of the transfer of learning. *Educational Psychologist, 14*, 53–69.

Salomon, G., & Perkins, D. N. (1989). Rocky roads to transfer: Rethinking mechanisms of a neglected phenomenon. *Educational Psychologist, 24*, 113–142.

Tannenbaum, S. I., & Yukl, G. (1992). Training and development in work organizations. *Annual Review of Psychology, 43*, 399–441.

Wexley, K. N., & Baldwin, T. T. (1986). Post-training strategies for facilitating positive transfer: An empirical exploration. *Academy of Management Journal, 29*, 503–520.

Willis, V. J., Deans, J., & Jones, H. (1998). Verifying themes in action learning: Implications for adult education and HRD. In R. J. Torraco (Ed.), *Academy of Human Resource Development Conference Proceedings* (pp. 497–505). Baton Rouge, LA: Academy of Human Resource Development.

Yorks, L., O'Neil, J., Marsick, V. J., Lamm, S., Kolodny, R., & Nilson, G. (1998). Transfer of learning from an action reflection learning program. *Performance Improvement Quarterly, 11*(1), 59–73.

Chapter 5

▲ Action Learning for Personal Development and Transformative Learning

Robert L. Dilworth
Verna J. Willis

> ***The Problem and the Solution.*** Organizations and those working in them have a serious problem keeping up with change. The renewal required to succeed is continuous. This chapter focuses on the practical aspects of the individual journey for personal development.

Action learning is increasingly being employed as a central strategy for organizational renewal by global corporations. The rapidly growing list of participating organizations includes GE, CONOCO, TRW, Whirlpool, National Semiconductor, Procter & Gamble, Unisys, and the Federal Deposit Insurance Corporation in Washington, D.C.

There are a number of reasons for this pronounced and accelerating shift to action learning approaches. Perhaps heading the list is frustration with traditional approaches to organizational change. The bandwagon effect also comes into play. As corporations such as GE enter their second decade of involvement with action learning and enjoy phenomenal growth in performance, productivity, and profitability, there is a strong inclination for others to experiment with this approach. Another factor spurring interest is the close alignment between the essence of action learning and the coalescence of corporate strategies around what are considered core drivers of competitive advantage. They include the need for transformative learning at both individual and organizational levels, flattening of organizations, boundarylessness (a fundamental goal at GE), new forms of leadership, empowerment of employees, the need for broad cross-functionality and integration of the enterprise, self-ordering systems, creation of learning organizations, and knowledge management.

With all the emphasis on change dynamics corporations and the need to transform corporate culture for global competitiveness, there is a growing appreciation of the importance of leadership at all levels in the corporate structure. Therefore, interest turns to personal development and transformative learning. There is an awareness that the education received in schools of business, engineering, and other analytically turned and highly systematized disciplines may not produce people who have the kinds of behaviors and understandings necessary for leadership today. Classical command and control leadership styles give way to more nurturing and noninterventionist styles of leadership, styles more befitting a self-directed work team environment.

What Is Transformative Learning?

Any time we learn something new and absorb it, either through life experience or an educational event, we are transformed in some way. It may be imperceptible to us and others, but our mental processes are in fact altered. Over time, these incremental changes can aggregate into a compelling reason for change. A good analogy is that of water building up behind a dam. It eventually either overflows or ruptures the dam, emerging as new lakes or streams.

Not all transformations are positive. We learn that in our adult world when we observe business executives losing their sense of confidence and self-worth. In some cases the transformation can lead to debilitation of the individual. In corporations, it can manifest itself as corporate burnout. By similar reasoning, personal development is not always positive, even though we hope it will be that. Personal development that can help us in our life experience is the goal. This kind of development is challenging for the learner. The example of an action learning program that follows captures the essence of what it is like to participate in this kind of experience.

An Action Learning Experience

In 1996 thirty-one individuals, with an average age of forty-four, met in England for an action learning experience. Among them were the chief executive officer of a company, a high-level government official, and the senior vice president for human resources for a major U.S. global company. Others had considerable senior-level consulting experience, owned their own business, or were employed by large organizations in a variety of capacities.

Participants came from the United States, Australia, and Canada. Some of the learning coaches at the British university that was hosting the event were British. It was also an unusual event in that some of the leading authorities on action learning in the world assembled in support of the experience, including Reginald W. Revans of England, whom many consider the father of action learning. Each participant was placed in one of five action learning groups, referred to as sets (some corporations call them learning labs). Each set had six or seven members. For two weeks, each set would intensively work on a critical problem. The problem was real and of deep concern to the major firm collaborating with this learning opportunity.

The members of each set came from different backgrounds, and almost no one had a background in the problem areas they were given to work on. Set composition was determined with care so that each set was representative in terms of nationality, gender, life experience, age, and learning styles (each participant had been administered the Honey-Mumford Learning Style Questionnaire).

Participants were distanced from problems in which they had expertise. Although all problems centered on one very large British client firm, the problems differed greatly (for example, one dealt with financial management and another with downsizing). No leaders were designated for individual sets, and each ended up operating as a self-directed work team, with leadership either collective or only transitorily involving a set member. The leadership role was usually in a facilitative capacity as the set worked through a given issue area.

What Happened?

Many of the participants expressed a sense of transformation at the conclusion of the experience. Some defined it as perhaps the most important event of their life. One individual said, "I am forever changed. I don't know why. What I do know is that I do not want to go back to the way I was."

Although there was a belief that significant learning might occur, including that related to positive personal development and leadership development, transformation of a high order was not one of the expectations, nor was this meant to be a therapy session. It seems evident now that most of the participants returned to their organizations refreshed and with a sense of greater life focus. Contacts with participants after the experience tend to confirm this. Individual participants sensed "dam bursting" taking place in themselves. The outcomes of this event line up rather well with what has occurred in corporations that have taken the time to experiment with and use action learning as an organizational development strategy and alternative to traditional formal training approaches.

What Contributed to the Transformative Learning?

The event, which was engineered and orchestrated by Dilworth and actively supported from a research perspective by Willis, had some unique characteristics. These characteristics can advance thinking, and they can be of value to corporations either currently involved with action learning or those contemplating such involvement.

The preparation for this experience was probably a contributor to the transformation that occurred. All participants were asked to submit no more than three pages of information about themselves beforehand. The first requirement was a one-page sketch of where they were in their life, with a photograph. It was not in resumé or abbreviated curriculum vitae style. They were asked to develop an honest one-page life essay. These essays ended up addressing successes, marriage failures, burnout, what they wanted most to happen in their lives, what excited them the most about their work, and feelings of disillusionment. Comments were wide ranging and highly self-revealing. To model the openness that would characterize the experience and the honesty involved, Dilworth included his own life essay as an example.

Individuals also were asked to submit a one-page statement on their expectations for the experience and previous involvement with action learning (which was also used in determining set composition). Few had previously been involved with action learning.

To help them understand the nature of action learning, a select group of writings on action learning, and from different perspectives, was provided to each registrant. They were also given a video on action learning, featuring an interview of Revans. A second video featured an interview of Jack Mezirow, professor emeritus at Teachers College, Columbia University, on transformative learning and perspective transformation.

Because participants knew something about each other, including which set they would be in and the nature of the problem the set had been given to address, contacts between set members began to occur well before departure for England. Such communication was primarily by telephone and e-mail since participants were widely dispersed.

Each participant kept a "learning journal" throughout the two-week experience. After the program, they were to turn in two essays. One essay addressed their personal learning experience; the other addressed their assessment of action learning and the group process as it unfolded.

We worked to answer ten major questions in analyzing participant essays:

1. What is the nature of the interpersonal dynamics that surfaced when action learning sets were operating?
2. How have participants perceived the experience?
3. When were people likely to be most fully engaged or least engaged?
4. When were participants puzzled or uncertain about themselves or about what was occurring?
5. What learning gaps did participants discover in themselves?
6. When did they feel most affirmed?
7. What constituted the most important learning moment or event, and why?
8. How did participants assess the quality of interpersonal associations and interactions with the client?
9. What did the action learning program organizers and orchestrators learn from the experience?
10. How does what occurred inform the design of future action learning programs in general and of specific programs of this type?

In writing the essay related to their personal learning experience, participants were asked to think of various critical incidents (such as when they were most engaged or most distanced). The surprise came when their comments created new critical incident categories based on the frequency of response. Unanticipated categories developed through qualitative analysis included insight gained, personal transformation, and comments related to "intensity" of the experience.

Because participant commentary in these essays provide a direct index to their thinking, some excerpts by category follow:

- Most engaged: "There is much about the experience which is difficult to express in words, such as the 'spirit' of action learning—being honest and open, valuing others, having courage, and developing self-confidence."
- Most distanced: "It was stressful because we saw and heard different things, even though we were all at the same meetings."
- Most affirmed: "What became most evident to me as a result of the entire European experience was how action learning can bridge gaps between people and create a true brotherhood."
- Feeling of uncertainty: "Because sets are small, autonomous, or semi-autonomous self-directed work teams, they must deal with the inevitable problems that all such teams face. All set members are equal in their sets; no one is the 'boss' or even 'in charge.' If someone is, the group is not engaged in action learning."
- Best work: "My role was the harmonizer mediating conflict between group members and offering clarification on points made by the group."
- Personal transformation: "Personal growth always comes through meeting challenges that either life or we ourselves place before us. I totally enjoyed sharing a room with myself for two weeks. I was good company and I even learned from myself!"
- Insight gained: "I came to England to learn about action learning. Along the way, I learned a lot about myself. I do not know how to fast-grow a tomato, but I do know how a group of seven—five representing the cream of American womanhood and two colonists thrown in—can find its way in just six days."
- Learning gaps: "Being open to new and different ideas is important. One cannot generate fresh questions unless one is open to thinking about things in new ways. Learning cannot take place in a vacuum. The interaction and dialogue with other set members is essential if action learning is to work."
- Interpersonal: "I have to admit that even though our conflicts with [participant] were often unpleasant and frustrating, they led to further questioning and understanding for me. At this point I am still left with more questions than answers, but I have grown from the experience."
- Cognitive: "Action learning encourages set members to reflect on what works and what doesn't, and why. Reflection is used by set members to form and test theories they create to generally describe what needs to be done, based on given circumstances for success."

- Future action: "A by-product of this experience includes self-development and self-analysis. My learning was significant!"
- Intensity: "Indeed, it was quite a learning experience. I enjoyed every conversation, and every interaction, particularly those in small discussion groups after class, with my colleagues. We asked questions until we were too exhausted to ask more."
- Assumption or opinion: "The bottom line of action learning is that its participants learn how to learn through their experiences in their sets and their application of what they learn in their sets and in situations outside their sets."
- Use of metaphors: "While action learning itself is not merely 'learning by doing' as many assume when they first hear the phrase, it is a part of action, an extraordinary sort of action or approach to learning, which can only be understood—its meaning only realized—by doing it. By analogy, it's like learning a second language. Like language, one can only learn to do action learning through becoming immersed in action learning itself."

What Does This Action Learning Experience Suggest?

This action learning experience suggests both vintage action learning and human nature. Because participants were out of their normal environment, several things occurred. Being in an unfamiliar place, dealing with an unfamiliar problem (only two of thirty-one were employed in the industry being examined), and being surrounded by unfamiliar colleagues produced a tonic effect. Their personal assumptions and life experiences did not necessarily line up well with the environment in which they found themselves. They had to examine their own beliefs and the assumptions undergirding them. There was also a comfort level living side by side with discomfort. Although the challenge was discomforting, there was also a freedom. Office politics were at a minimum three thousand miles away. The participants could be themselves. They found that they were asking themselves and others fresh questions.

It can be posited that renewal requires turning your back on the mainstream of your life and looking at new scenery through fresh eyes. Like our peripheral vision at night, we are able to see better when we do not look at an object directly. As a result, we are better able to know who we are, where we are, and where we want to go.

What Can This Experience Tell Us About Action Learning in Companies?

This experience suggests that companies need to examine how they go about designing an action learning experience. Rather than assemble colleagues for action learning from the same division, office, or company, there is a case for removing people from their familiar environments and having them work with unfamiliar colleagues, including people from other companies. There is also a case for having them deal with unfamiliar problems, but that can be tough to sell to the leaders in corporations. ("You mean you are sending Charlie to Peoria to study issues related to how shopping centers can be better designed? Get off it. That has nothing to do with our bottom line.")

Another lesson is that intensive time blocks can work better than interrupted time blocks. If a participant works outside the area for a day or two and then returns to the home office, only to sally forth once again to do action learning two weeks later, he or she can never really get loose from his or her existing thought process. It is also stressful to juggle a corporate workload and then tear away from it briefly as it builds up.

Those selected to participate must understand that they have no status in the set. All individuals are equal.

Finally, the project has to be in real time and genuine. It is not a puzzle to be solved, a case study, or fabrication of a make-work project. It must be real, and it must be challenging, with a clear expectation that the set will bring substantial recommendations and solutions to the table.

When all these factors are brought together, magic can occur. It happened in England in 1996. Two years later, many of the participants continue to be in contact, with set "reunions" planned. To have such a powerful connection made after such a brief period of engagement suggests the depth of the experience.

Chapter 6

▲ Organizational Culture Change Through Action Learning

Glenn E. Nilson

> ***The Problem and the Solution.*** Many people talk about culture change in organizations, but what exactly is meant by this? This chapter lays out the components of organizational culture and culture change through action learning, as well as how the components relate to practice.

Transformational organization change is generally assumed to involve changing an organization's culture. However, the social processes of that culture change have received little formal attention. This chapter examines the way in which an action learning program has been used to drive a desired culture change into an organization that is attempting to develop globalization of the perspectives and behaviors of its international business units. The form of action learning used to achieve this change was critical reflection. The theoretical model that is described demonstrates how learning triggered by the action learning intervention produced such a culture change and highlights the important components of that change process. The practical implications of the model for those seeking to foster similar changes are provided.

Organizational Culture

Culture is typically conceived as a system of shared meanings, values, and behavioral expectations. It is usually considered to be the major determinant of individuals' behavior within organizations, and it has often been treated as a managerial product that can be introduced, cascaded, and diffused within an organization to result in whatever system of values and behaviors is desired. In fact, Schein (1985) regards culture manipulation as the prime responsibility of management. Culture change can be mishandled by managers as well (Deal & Kennedy, 1982), as, for example, when a new CEO introduces a change that undermines important existing values or destroys the position of a company hero. Deal and Kennedy (1982) assert that successful managers of the future will be those "who can forge the values and beliefs" of the organization. Thus, shaping and maintaining the desired culture of an organization is asserted to be the ultimate responsibility of management (Deal & Kennedy, 1982, p. 193).

In this regard, management arguably affects the character of individual behavior within an organization when it sets the organization's cultural norms and values. When management wishes to change the organization's culture, and hence the behavior of its employees, it can attempt to introduce new values and behavioral norms in various ways, including issuing policies, behavioral directives, and using training programs. However, practical experience informs us that policies, directives, and training programs do not always translate into desired organizational and behavioral changes. In common experience, organizational change is not a simple linear process accomplished through management intentions and initiatives.

While intentional organizational change is accepted to imply organizational culture change, this chapter takes a less deterministic approach and views culture change as more socially constructed than managerially determined. As Trice and Beyer (1993, p. 5) note,

> Cultures cannot be produced by individuals acting alone. They originate as individuals interact with one another. Individuals may originate specific ways of managing the fundamental insecurities of life, but until these specific ways come to be collectively accepted and put into practice, they are not part of a culture.

Culture derives from the collective interpretation and designation of events that symbolize important (and sometimes emergent) values, perspectives, and behavioral roles (Fine, 1979). The organization's culture is constantly being defined (or reiterated) as people interact and respond to daily events. These interpreted and designated events contribute to the system of meanings that in part make up the organization's culture. Thus, a training program, or the promulgation of a policy or directive, is not a pure agent that determines culture; rather it is an event that may affect the organization's culture depending on how employees interpret it.

As an example, new behavior transferred through a training program and required by management may be interpreted and defined as simply the same old authoritarianism that has existed all along, and not be defined as signifying a new basis for social interaction. If, on the other hand, behavior transferred through a training program is collectively defined as introducing and symbolizing a new social basis for social action, then the organization's culture can be said to be changing. The organization will reflect that change in the shared understandings that emerge to interpret what the organization is and how people within it are expected to behave. On the other hand, if the event is interpreted as another authoritarian demand, then the organization's culture will simply be reinforced through this interpretation, along the lines of the status quo. The transfer of learning will not have accomplished a change in the organization's culture.

From this perspective, an organization's culture can be seen as a matrix of socially shared and significant understandings that its members use to determine what things that happen mean in the context of the organization's culture and how people can be expected to behave. Thus, acquiring new behavior is only one part, or aspect, of culture change; assigning new socially shared meanings to events and behavior is another significant part of constructing the organization's culture differently.

An organization's culture is a collective means of mitigating against uncertainty and a means to "channel people's actions so that most of the time [people] repeat apparently successful patterns of behavior" (Trice & Beyer, 1993, p. 2). Thus, an organization's culture is as much a response of its members to situations they encounter, or have imposed on them, as it is a product of managerial ideas and directives. Rather than organizational culture being viewed as determined by management and diffused throughout the organization, in this chapter the culture of the organization is viewed as a product of the interaction of members of the organization at all levels. Organizational change, far from being a linear and unidirectional process, stems from the emergence of new behavior grounded in new socially constructed and shared meanings and behavior expectations, and it is an aspect of culture change. It is holistic and organic.

The significance for understanding intentional organizational change from this perspective of an organization's culture is that it becomes necessary to look at the dynamics of social interaction that ultimately produce, or change, the organization's culture. This approach does not ignore the important role of leadership or management in the construction or change of culture, but it gives more weight to the significance of what Argyis and Schön (1978) refer to as "theories in practice" over "espoused theories."

In a stable situation, culture is the taken-for-granted meanings and meta-language, together with shared values and behavioral expectations, that provide a basis for individuals to meet problems and take actions individually while remaining socially coordinated. In such a stable situation, organizational participants maintain established values, definitions, and behavioral expectations, and assign meanings consistent with the existing culture to newly encountered events. In effect, they recreate the organization's established culture in their everyday behavior. In a changing or unstable context, social behavior is focused on constructing a new and shared definition of the situation, that is, new meanings, which will again enable individuals to orient their behavior collectively. In changing situations, participants develop new elements to modify the organization's culture.

From this perspective, there are important questions to be addressed when an organization undertakes intentional change, as, for example, when a consultant is brought in with a program to accomplish specific change objectives. How do program objectives become incorporated into the organization's culture as a set of shared meanings and taken-for-granted values, beliefs, and assumptions? How do program participants introduce these changes into the organization as culture change elements, and how do they become socially accepted as culture change and as new behavioral expectations? In other words, how does behavior, which is called for in the context of a training setting, become part of the day-to-day behavior socially expected in the larger organization?

Components of Culture Change Observed from an Action Learning Program

The model described in this section is derived from data gathered through seventy-one formal interviews conducted throughout a company, field notes taken by a participant observer throughout the program, and many "opportunistic interviews" with participants during the program (ARL Inquiry, 1995a, 1995b).

Analysis of the available data suggested that four components of culture change occur through action learning. These components, along with their effects, are summarized in Table 6.1. The first, *Exhibiting Cultural Components*, was the appearance in the everyday work behavior of the organization's members, new behaviors, values, and attitudes that reflected participation in the intervention. The second component, *Symbolizing Cultural Components*, occurred when new behavior and changed perspectives were given meaning and communicated among organization members. The third, *Sanctioning Cultural Components*, indicated that members received social support and reinforcement for exhibiting these attitudes, values, and behaviors. The fourth, *Reinforcing and Refining New Cultural Components*, referred to individuals' reviewing and refining the new values and behaviors within a group or network of change participants. These four process components—Exhibiting, Symbolizing, Sanctioning, and Reinforcing and Refining—are presented as a theoretical model pertaining to the incorporation of change through action learning into an organization's culture. Closer examination of what these process components mean will highlight their contributions as elements of a culture change process.

Exhibiting Cultural Components

This change component, Exhibiting, means that new behaviors become known, accepted, and displayed among members of the organization. The action learning program studied emphasized developing interaction skills and values in addition to globalization. Therefore, it was necessary to look for evidence of globalization and other new interaction skills and perspectives. One early indication of globalization outside the intervention setting came when members of different business units began cooperating and using each other as resources, replacing previous practices of individual company competition. Another is reflected in changes in interpersonal communication following participation in the intervention experience. One participant described these changes as follows:

> When you go through the intervention, it's the idea of a shared adversity creating a bond between people. Certainly all of us have a more intimate

▲ **Table 6.1 Culture Change Model Components and Effects**

Components of Change	Component Definitions	Component Effects
Exhibiting cultural components	Introducing new values and behaviors into everyday practices	Diffuses learned perspectives and behaviors into existing cultural context
Symbolizing cultural components	Naming and defining new values and behaviors in terms of organizational implications and acceptance	Makes communication of new values and behaviors, together with their organizational significance, feasible
Sanctioning cultural components	Modeling of new values and behaviors by organizational leaders and members and attributing positive results to their use	Incorporates new cultural components within the reward structure of the organization
Reinforcing and refining cultural components	Repeated expression and use of new values and behaviors, with possible modification to fit the organization's needs	Maintains and furthers accepted use of components, and uniquely adapts them to the organization

> relationship in the business sense with each other. That kind of intimacy, I guess it's based on trust; you're more open and more direct, and it has great benefits in communication with the organization. The ability to pick up the phone to talk to someone you haven't talked to in six months—you are immediately at a higher level of communication than you would be if it was just a person you happen to know on a functional basis through the organization. I've seen and experienced the benefits of that, and there are a lot of people who were involved in a project and came out to our facility. It would have never have happened if there hadn't been communication, if it had just been between managers. We provided a lot of assistance to them, knowing full well that this doesn't benefit the profit and loss statement of my business unit. It's a global organization project.

From these comments we see that both the level of trust and interpersonal knowledge gained as a result of participating in the action learning program influenced the subsequent likelihood that interaction would take place among different members and companies within this organization. It is also clear that other individuals who were not part of the program directly started participating in events that crossed previous organization boundaries. Most important, we learn that this changed behavior is not driven by previously existing values and norms—the potential for profit to one's own company—but by the introduction of a new way of defining situations as global organization opportunities.

As a result of participating in the program, personnel began viewing direct interpersonal communication and cooperation as behavior that had become the way members of the company now expected to handle problems and conduct business. Their behavior *exhibited* changed values. As a perspective, globalization had come to mean interacting and cooperating across boundaries that had traditionally separated departments, divisions, companies, and individuals. Cooperation across traditional boundaries was exhibited and recognized as a new corporate value. Comment by members of the organization were similar to this one:

> I guess the biggest impact I've seen has been the fact that we definitely seem to have become one company. Prior to the action learning program, trying to get information was difficult. I've seen 100 percent improvement, and it's

even better than probably 100 percent. If I have a problem or question and know someone who has a solution to that, I don't see any barriers to my being able to call that person up and getting that information. Two years ago, it didn't happen. We tried, and you couldn't do it.

Symbolizing Cultural Components

The second culture change component is that new behaviors, attitudes, and values are given meaning and made communicable among the organization's members. There were two ways in which this took place. Members of the organization developed a jargon to use in reference to the action learning program, or some aspect of it, and they began using terms they learned in the program to designate certain behaviors in the everyday workplace.

During early observations of the second action learning program, the observer noted that participants initially made comments about having seen participants in the first program return, appearing to have been through some sort of religious conversion experience. These comments seemed to express participants' expectations that monumental personal changes would be expected on the part of the learning coaches, and they also expressed their concern that the intervention was a threat to the existing culture. However, references to spiritual conversion died out and did not reappear in subsequent programs, and there were fewer expressions of doubt or fear about the nature or expected benefits to be derived by participating in action learning.

Adoption of the principles of action learning grew and changed, as did the ways in which organizational members defined and symbolized the event. This illustrates the ongoing nature of building an organization's cultural responses to situations being encountered. Participants in early programs seemed to be groping for a means of capturing their learning experience. Symbols that were carried directly from the intervention experience and were used to communicate the program-based values and practices came mostly from techniques introduced in the program. One interviewee commented that "it's generated a bit of a language that has helped recognize situations."

One of the techniques taught in the program, reflection and dialogue (R&D), was often discussed or mentioned by interviewees:

Some of the managers have implemented the reflection dialogue technique and they do it on a regular basis and make sure they try to stick to it, because they obviously try to improve communication and get the people who are actually doing the day-to-day work, get their input.

Sanctioning Cultural Components

The third culture change component was that members gave and received mutual support and reinforcement for exhibiting the new cultural behaviors. In the following example, a technique taught in the program, called "stop-and-reflect," was invoked in an everyday work situation:

> I was at a meeting with a member of the executive team. I got a little excited; he got a little excited. And then he said, "Oh, let's do a stop and reflect. Let's take five minutes right now, where we are here." I thought, that's neat. Came back in five minutes later and found that there really weren't as many issues as we thought there were and we got to some closure pretty quickly. He never would have done that a year before.

Support for new behaviors resulted from modeling them, as well as from making positive comments about them. It also came from participating in an event in which the new behavior was used and then recognizing the event as having gone better than previous similar ones had.

Support through modeling is particularly important when it comes from superiors. Since the participants in the action learning program were high-level executives, their transfer of new behaviors into everyday practice can be assumed to have had a generally positive effect on the way those working under them viewed the culture as changing. An example is provided by the following observation of changes in the behaviors of other executives who went through the program and gave recognition to a conscious effort to model, and thus sanction, the new desired behaviors.

> Individuals I think have changed. [Name of a vice president] has done a really good job of taking to heart the teachings of the program. In trying to, in becoming a more sensitive manager, I think [names another executive] has some good work and things like that. I think our leader, who hasn't actually

gone through the program, struggles with control and hands-off a lot. I've seen, literally seen, him tell himself to shut up.

Reinforcing and Refining Cultural Components

The fourth culture change component occurred when individuals who shared the behaviors, and their social meanings, reviewed and possibly refined them within a group or network of participants. This component was reflected in participants' observations concerning conditions needed to make the change happen, as well as observations of things being done. An important means of reinforcing the use of new behaviors was simply the number of people who would understand them and think they were worthwhile.

As participants attempted to introduce behavioral changes into the organization, it helped when they could point out instances of others' using them, perhaps unconsciously, and discuss the implications and impact of behaving differently. Discussion of such instances is a means by which new cultural components explicitly become social property:

> There are informal groups formed because of the program. I have as an example that people sit together with the finance guy and the production guy and say that this is not the way it should go and let's do something about it. We sit together and try to define some sort of strategy because going one step higher doesn't make any sense. So now some things are moving, and because there are more people involved, the groups are getting bigger, and there are more disciples within the organization who have the same ideas and same feelings.

Summary of the Culture Change Process

Organizational change that resulted from the action learning intervention began with a program for executives that offered participants skills and techniques in interaction and new values and perspectives. The overt thrust of this program was to generate globalism as part of the organization's culture. Additional effects of the program focused on creating an environment in which participating executives could learn interaction techniques and perspectives that would foster and use trust, cooperation, and communication among the various companies that made up this international organization.

The impact of the program on participants was generally positive and dramatic, although the new behaviors were not accepted immediately. Initial reactions were hesitant, and new behaviors were met with skepticism in the larger organization. Initial participants embracing the program were defined as having experienced a religious-like conversion. However, as additional programs were accomplished, participation was redefined as providing a positive experience and contributing worthwhile values and ideas. Participants began modeling the techniques they had learned and exhibiting the changed values they had acquired as a result of the intervention experience. These changed attitudes and behaviors were symbolized by reference to named events and techniques, and provided a special language to share and diffuse the intervention change throughout the existing culture.

The diffusion of the change was reinforced by opportunities to discuss and use the new attitudes and behaviors among those who shared the background experience and common language. Organizational acceptance of the change was reinforced through modeling new behaviors and positively sanctioning the use of new behaviors on the part of others, especially management.

Implications for Practice

Corporate change interventions generally incorporate some sort of structural change or training program intended to produce organizational outcomes of a desired nature. Corporate culture change is typically attempted in a top-down manner with an assumption that designing and modifying the organization's culture is an executive capability and, indeed, responsibility. Little attention has been given to the social nature and processes of organizational culture construction and modification. Often training programs and structural changes fail to produce desired changes in everyday practice, especially in the long run.

The results of this study indicate that new values and behaviors are introduced into the organization by individuals who model and communicate desired changes in everyday work situations. Furthermore, the utility and efficacy of these new practices are weighed and communicated as part of the social change process.

Several implications from these observations seem evident. First, the desired culture change behaviors must be readily performable and observable. The desired change should be readily communicable and discussible among intervention participants and other members of the organization who will be constructing the new culture. This may help explain the popularity and success of training programs that incorporate easy-to-phrase, remember, and communicate principles.

The desired change must be usable within the context of everyday work situations, and its use must be rewarded. The proving ground for a change intervention is in the everyday workplace and within everyday interaction, not aside from it. Training programs often end at the close of the formal training session, but results of this study indicate that although personal change may take place within a training session, organizational culture change takes place within the social context of everyday behavior.

Action learning, because of its design, is especially well suited to being included in the arsenals of change agents that seek transformational change in an organization's culture. Accomplishing this kind of change requires that those sponsoring the program incorporate components of culture change into their program.

First, specific linkages need to be made between the processes used in the program and the work setting. Action learning programs designed with cycles between formal program meetings, project work, and work back in the organization are well suited for building these linkages. Second, participants in the program must include visible leaders who can model and reward desired changes, sanctioning them in the organization. Third, desired actions and behaviors must be named in ways that make them clearly recognizable. Fourth, those who are trying to get the change accomplished in the organization must prepare its climate to support critical reflection on the assumptions embedded in its existing culture and reward behavior in everyday practice that comes out of the reflection process. This requires close collaboration among those sponsoring the effort in the organization and those designing the program.

References

Argyris, C., & Schön, D. A. (1978). *Organizational learning: A theory of action perspective*. Reading, MA: Addison-Wesley.

ARL Inquiry. (1995a). Designing action reflection learning research: Balancing research needs and real-world constraints. In E. Holton III (Ed.), *Academy of Human Resource*

Development Proceedings (pp. 2–3). Baton Rouge, LA: Academy of Human Resource Development.

ARL Inquiry. (1995b). Life on the seesaw: Tensions in an action reflection learning program. *Adult Education Research Conference Proceedings* (pp. 1–6). University of Alberta, Edmonton, Alberta, Canada.

Deal, T. E., & Kennedy, A. A. (1982). *Corporate cultures: The rites and rituals of corporate life.* Reading, MA: Addison-Wesley.

Fine, G. (1979). Small groups and culture creation: The idioculture of Little League baseball teams. *American Sociological Review, 44,* 733–745.

Schein, E. H. (1985). *Organizational culture and leadership.* San Francisco: Jossey-Bass.

Trice, H. M., & Beyer, J. M. (1993). *The cultures of work organizations.* Englewood Cliffs, NJ: Prentice Hall.

Chapter 7

▲ Lessons for Implementing Action Learning

Lyle Yorks
Victoria J. Marsick
Judy O'Neil

> *The Problem and the Solution.* How do you pull off an action learning initiative? This chapter brings it all together while providing additional considerations for professional understanding and practice. In addition, the issues of assessment and the larger topic of organizational learning are covered.

In Chapter One we met Susan, a human resource development professional who was trying to make sense out of the choices confronting her company in initiating an action learning program: which approach to take; what program design to adopt; how to develop learning coaches, including whether to use internal or external resources in this role; how to go about training coaches; and issues around personal development and changing the culture of the organization. Another set of questions that confronts Susan is how to assess the learning from whatever program is put in place and how to position action learning to produce organizational change.

In this chapter we highlight the lessons of previous chapters in order to provide a framework for these choices. We suggest ways to position action learning for transformational organizational change and ways to assess learning outcomes.

Choosing an Action Learning Approach

Different action learning approaches—tacit, scientific, experiential, or critical reflection— produce different outcomes and help to achieve different objectives. Action learning programs can also produce noise in the organization. All those collaborating in the change effort need to make informed choices when they select an approach and a design.

Exhibit 7.1 is a decision table to guide these choices based on the discussion in Chapter One and the action learning pyramid in Figure 1.1. The first column of the table raises basic questions about organizational readiness for action learning. "Yes" answers to these questions are necessary for implementing action learning regardless of the school. The second and third columns raise questions that provide for differentiation among the four schools. The suggested school in the fourth column is the one that would generally be the best fit.

Some caveats are in order. First, the questions in this exhibit are a starting point. They are not prescriptive but rather will trigger reflection, suggest additional data gathering, and aid in decision making. For this reason, the column on the far right is intended to encourage reflective comment on choices and assumptions.

Susan, her colleagues, and representatives of the line organization could use this exhibit to answer the questions, reflect on the assumptions and data on which their answers are based, and then have a dialogue among themselves to resolve differing perceptions and decide next steps. They might present choices to management and others, conduct a more complete needs analysis, and clarify learning expectations. Based on these activities, they will have to make reflective judgments about advocating action learning.

Second, although the questions in the exhibit are closed-ended and may seem deterministic, they are designed to stimulate thinking and conversation that will uncover further nuances. Choices may lead initially to a scientific design, but discussion could show a strong need to consider the personal development of participants, which would push designers toward a different approach. As programs are initiated, further changes ensue. For example, an experiential program may morph into critical reflection as the organization becomes more tolerant of the noise produced by action learning, and management comes to see its role in different terms.

The questions in the first column are basic to any action learning effort. Action learning programs assume that managers are confronted by compelling unstructured problems—problems that require Q learning. They also assume a willingness to consider generative solutions. If the

▲ Exhibit 7.1 Decision Table for Choosing an Action Learning Approach

Basic Questions (Answers Must All Be Yes)	Secondary Questions (Selecting an Approach)	If . . . (Contingency)	Most Appropriate Action Learning Response	Comments (Additional Considerations, Concerns)
Are managers and/or the organization confronted with compelling, unstructured questions?	a) Does the organization have a highly directive leadership culture that it doesn't wish challenged?			
Do members of the organization generally accept the need for improved organizational learning?	b) Are the desired learning outcomes centered around developing strategic thinking and/or answers to strategic questions?	If the answer to *a* and *b* is yes, then. . . .	Tacit	

If team approach, are leaders prepared to act as project sponsors?	c) In addition to *b* above, do desired formal learning outcomes include problem reframing, problem setting, and the learning of a problem resolution process?	If the answer to *a* is no and to *c* is yes, then. . . . Scientific
	d) In addition to *b* and *c* above, do desired formal learning outcomes include personal development of participants?	If the answer to *a* is no and to *d* is yes, then. . . . Experiential
	e) In addition to *b* and *c* above, do desired learning outcomes include transformational individual and organizational learning?	If the answer to *a* is no and to *e* is yes, then go to *f*, *g*, and *h* below.

(Continued)

Exhibit 7.1 Decision Table for Choosing an Action Learning Approach (continued)

Basic Questions (Answers Must All Be Yes)	Secondary Questions (Selecting an Approach)	If . . . (Contingency)	Most Appropriate Action Learning Response	Comments (Additional Considerations, Concerns)
	f) Is management prepared to accept a high level of uncertainty and ambiguity around learning outcomes?	If yes, go to *h*. If no, consider experiential approach.	Experiential	
	g) Is there sufficient organizational justification for generating a high level of organizational noise?	If yes, go to *h*. If no, consider experiential approach.	Experiential	
	h) Are senior leaders prepared to learn?	If yes, then. . . .	Critical reflection	

program is going to involve team projects, organizational leaders who are more senior than the participants must be prepared to sponsor projects.

A key consideration is the nature of the organization's leadership culture. If leaders are highly directive and they do not wish to change this style, then the tacit approach may be the most appropriate. The tacit approach allows people to learn incidentally and to address organizational issues without creating excessive noise that is counter to the culture. Project questions lead to desired learning outcomes and better strategic thinking.

As the pyramid model in Figure 1.1 suggests, the scientific approach is most appropriate when participants are also expected to gain skills in problem setting, problem reframing, and problem resolution. If personal development is as important as problem setting, then the experiential approach edges out the more scientific approach, primarily because of the advantages of more continuing involvement of the learning coach.

The critical reflection model is the best choice when the organization wants transformational learning for individuals and the organization. Key issues to consider include whether management is prepared for the uncertainty and the level of noise that is likely to be generated by this approach, whether senior managers are prepared to accept their own need for learning as part of the process, and whether the human resource development specialists are ready to accept the challenges to the initiative that the program is likely to generate initially. A certain degree of noise will accompany any action learning intervention, but it is likely to be more intense at the top of the pyramid because of the program's objectives and design.

Once initiators are clear on what approach best approximates their needs and can articulate the reasons, they are in a position to select coaches and make decisions around program design, if appropriate. Their choices will frame what they seek in a learning coach, the kind of reflection they will try to encourage in the program, and the kind of content, or *P* learning, that is provided.

Choosing an Action Learning Program Design

In Chapter Two, O'Neil and Dilworth raise issues of importance relative to program design: the mix of familiar and unfamiliar in the setting and the problem and the use of individual or team projects in the program. Table 7.1 summarizes some key issues surrounding these two design

▲ **Table 7.1 Key Design Characteristics: A Summary**

Design Characteristic	Potential Advantages	Potential Disadvantages	Comments
Familiar setting/familiar problem	High and immediate relevance for participants; can be individual or team problem	Participants may recreate existing patterns of thinking and interacting; if team problem, can easily become a task force rather than a learning group	Use of learning coach is advisable; scientific or experiential model most likely, although critical reflection possible if organization is prepared
Unfamiliar setting/unfamiliar problem	Potential for producing deep learning; most likely to produce transformational learning regardless of approach; team problem	If tacit approach is used once group dynamics are established, learning will be primarily on the problem	High potential for critical reflection approach
Unfamiliar setting/familiar problem	Can challenge existing organizational practices; team problem	Participants may not sufficiently focus on contextual issues, developing more of a "best-practices" mentality; can get caught in not-invented-here syndrome on part of client system	Learning coach can raise contextual issues; experiential approach very appropriate

Familiar setting/ unfamiliar problem	Can lead to solutions to very vexing problems; can be individual or team problem	Organization may not be prepared for the solutions; may resent the "intrusion" of privileged learners	Role of sponsors is very important, and learning coaches must be prepared to coach them
Individual problems	Leads to improved individual practice	Participant may become increasingly critical of work context	At minimum, learning coaches necessary at start of set
Organizational problems	Leads to organizational change and improved organizational performance	Task can more easily drive out learning	Approach and projects must be appropriate for the organizational culture and context

points. The third is choice of participants, and the fourth, the length and spacing of time in the program.

Settings and Problems: Familiar Versus Unfamiliar

Participants will more easily see the relevance of the program to their job when they work in a familiar setting and on a familiar problem. However, they may also fall into familiar patterns of thinking and interaction and unintentionally recreate the dynamics that have made the problem so difficult to resolve in the first place. Working in a familiar setting on a familiar problem can also lead to a task force mentality as opposed to a learning orientation. Use of a learning coach throughout the program to encourage questioning and reflection can help avoid these potential disadvantages.

Placing participants in an unfamiliar setting to deal with unfamiliar problems will produce the deepest learning. As Dilworth and Willis argue in Chapter Five, unfamiliarity helps people think in new patterns and might cause them to recognize and challenge their assumptions. This is an added advantage when participants are also working on a strategic organizational issue. Even if the program is based on the tacit approach, participants will be confronted with new ways of understanding the situation because everything about it is so different.

When the problem is familiar but the setting is unfamiliar, new ideas are likely to ensue because people will import their favorite practices from outside the organization. This may result in defensiveness around the not-invented-here syndrome. Participants could also try to import a practice without recognizing the need to adapt it because of differences in context. Active learning coaches can help to avoid these problems.

The familiar setting–unfamiliar problem mix is often used in business units and profit centers. Team members are drawn from functional areas other than the one most central to the problem. As O'Neil and Dilworth have cautioned, this option can lead teams to suggest highly generative actions that the organization is not prepared to support. Unless a strong sponsor is prepared to advocate on behalf of the teams, the preconditions of critical reflection school are a good safeguard here.

Individual or Organizational Problems

A key question should be answered in making the choice between using personal problems or team problems in the program. Is the purpose of the program to help participants to be more effective in their personal practice within the organizational context, or is the purpose oriented more to organizational change? When team projects are used, it is wise to give careful consideration to the organizational culture and the extent to which the core culture of the organization can be challenged. The relationship between team and sponsor is also crucial. Learning coaches can help, but they need access to sponsors, and they need to assess the degree to which sponsors are prepared to challenge existing organizational norms.

When the focus is on individual projects, the gains relate more to individual capacity building. This can be accomplished through the scientific, experiential, or critical reflection approaches. At a minimum, learning coaches are necessary to help the group to work together more effectively using the action learning process. The critical reflection approach is most likely to make participants unhappy with existing organizational arrangements and initiate challenges to management.

Selecting Participants and Program Timing

Participants should be selected for a program within the context of an ongoing development plan. The issue of volunteers versus nonvolunteers needs to be resolved. If the intention is critical reflection, more senior people should be involved in the program, before including people from the middle and lower levels. The rationale should be self-evident: this kind of learning should start at the top and work its way down the organization.

The balancing of costs and participant availability against desired outcomes influences choices about the amount of time invested in action learning. These decisions affect the learning that takes place in the program and the degree to which learning can be transferred back to the job. Extended learning experiences, spaced over time, facilitate the process of learning transfer.

Learning Transfer and Culture Change

In Chapter Six, Nilson describes the way in which action learning can trigger organizational culture change. We think that programs oriented to critical reflection are most likely to lead to this transformation. However, if they are to be effective, the organization should plan from the start for learning transfer and for addressing steps to culture change.

Positioning action learning as part of a larger change strategy is especially important in transformational change. We have found that action learning can act as a catalyst for organizational transformation (ARL Inquiry, 1997) by creating something akin to a liberating structure within the organization that stimulates interaction among several factors needed for this kind of change. A liberating structure is "a kind of organizing that is productive and at the same time educates its members toward self-correcting awareness" (Fisher & Torbert, 1995, p. 7; see also Torbert, 1991). The program acts as a "container" of sorts, or a safe space, within which strategic change can be implemented. Participants can revise, refine, and experiment with strategy. They can design systems and structures, and identify changes in practices necessary for the change to succeed.

An example from the global food company highlighted in Chapters Four and Six will show how this is possible. One project in this company was defined as follows: "What *radical changes* can be made within [the company's] financial and administrative areas that will significantly *reduce costs* while providing acceptable levels of internal control and improving *service to internal and external customers* to the highest level?" In this team's report to their sponsor, they noted that the need for change is rooted in the "changing environment . . . and [we] must become more customer and market driven due to increased global competition." The project team understood an important question underlying the project to be: "How can [the finance function] become a strategic weapon by being a source of strength not possessed by our competitors?" The team recommended changes in the way in which the financial function was organized on a global basis and the kinds of systems necessary to make it work. The team's recommendations also included significant learning centered around the following insights: (1) a new understanding of the changing environment, (2) the acceptance of the strategy of globalization, (3) the necessity of thinking strategically about globalization, (4) changes in both structure and system, and (5) new competencies necessary for functioning in a global context.

These changes did not take place in a vacuum; the team followed steps taken by management to articulate a vision of globalization, supported by a business case argument. This vision was reinforced by a search conference, through which managers diagnosed their existing organizational culture as running counter to this new vision. An organizational culture survey was also conducted that, among other things, identified specific competencies that were lacking in the organization to achieve the vision.

The exact nature of the specific steps is less important than the overall dynamic of integrated change. Prior to action learning, management made a business case for change, built a base of support for that strategic change, and provided evidence from the organization itself on the need for learning. Following the action learning effort, as Nilson (Chapter Six) has documented, management continued to sanction and reinforce the competencies developed in the program. Developmental feedback on the core competencies continued to be provided as well, increasing the probability of learning transfer. In short, the action learning program was linked to an ongoing process of change involving other interventions known to be useful in transformational change efforts. These were followed by subsequent initiatives that targeted learning transfer and culture change.

Links to Organizational Learning

Organizational learning, and the development of a learning organization, is a subject that has been addressed by a number of authors (Marquardt, 1996; Marsick & Watkins, forthcoming; Senge, 1990; Watkins & Marsick, 1993). Most of these authors agree that individual and team learning play a significant role in helping to create a learning organization. As we have seen in this book, action learning can be used to leverage both individual and team learning, which can help create organizational learning. Action learning helps to build a critical mass of change agents who influence larger-scale change. Action learning represents a significant organizational intervention that can release considerable energy for change into the organization.

The connections between action learning and organizational learning can be fairly obvious. What is less obvious is the reason that organizational learning is important. Using action learning to bring about change and organizational learning, and to help create a learning organization, is a significant undertaking. It is important for the organization to understand the benefits; otherwise, the effort may not receive the support it needs to be effective.

Marsick and Watkins (forthcoming) have presented a sound rationale for the importance of organizational learning. They discuss the connections joining learning, knowledge, intellectual capital, and business results:

> Our model [for a learning organization] emphasizes three key components: 1) systems-level, continuous learning; 2) that is created in order to create and manage knowledge outcomes; 3) which lead to improvement in the organization's performance, and ultimately its value, as measured through both financial assets and non-financial intellectual capital. Learning helps people to create and manage knowledge that builds a system's intellectual capital. Recent research confirms the links among these three components.

Marsick and Watkins create a case for a strong link between the kind of learning that can be generated from an action learning initiative and the processes of a learning organization. As an integral part of an overall change effort, action learning can contribute significantly to the creation of organizational learning and improved organizational results.

In the northeastern utility company, ongoing evaluation has shown evidence of individual and team learning. An organizational evaluation demonstrated results of systems-level continuous learning as well. In response to interview questions that asked if they had seen changes in the organization as a result of the initiative, up to 79 percent of participants interviewed responded that they had:

> Yes, I think that people are starting to believe that upper and middle management want people to express their feelings and ideas. The message that is being sent forth is that when people speak up, they are being praised.

Yes, I do see it starting to happen; the learning is taking effect. We are starting to get complete buy-in on our learning, and I am starting to see that happening both inside and outside the department.

> We are not a lot of hotheads anymore. We are acting more grown up, more mature, more professional. We are using more of the reflection part of the program.

Marsick and Watkins (forthcoming) provide a basis for understanding why this systems-level continuous and organizational learning occurred. They describe four action imperatives that support learning at the organizational level: (1) establishing systems that capture and share learning, (2) empowering people toward a collective vision, (3) connecting the organization to its environment, and (4) providing strategic leadership for learning. The utility company engaged in activities in support of their action learning initiative that fit with these action imperatives. The action learning program took place in a context in which these imperatives were created around the program. Action learning programs can function as a catalyst for learning organization initiatives; alone they will not result in a learning organization (ARL Inquiry, 1997).

Assessing the Learning

Assessment of learning can be an important part of organizational change. We make a distinction between assessing return on investment in terms of project outcomes and assessment of the learning that takes place as a result of the project work and, where appropriate, personal development.

Business return on project work can be assessed in both quantitative and qualitative terms. It is possible to track the dollar savings or revenue enhancement value as a result of changes implemented in traditional quantitative ways. Qualitatively, senior managers can make judgments about the contribution of changes that teams make to the organization's performance. For example, in one organization, the projects resulted in increased customer focus and contact. Although no immediate dollar savings were associated with these changes, senior management saw the value of increased customer satisfaction. The project built goodwill, and that helped the company realize its marketing strategy.

Assessing learning is a different matter. Some of the best measures of learning are found in reported evidence that demonstrate a difference in how participants think, their schema, and critical actions. One of the ways to capture this is through the use of critical incidents. Critical incidents can be captured in writing or orally through self-report. Participants can be asked to provide a one- or two-paragraph description of an event of significance to them. Oral reports may provide better evidence because they avoid a tendency in writing toward generalities and allow an interviewer to probe for detail. This method has been used successfully at the utility company. Self-report incidents can be triangulated with similar critical incident interviews with managers,

> ▲ **Exhibit 7.2 Sample Critical Incident Questions**
>
> *For participant*
> Think back to a critical incident that has happened on the job since you finished participating in the action learning program. Describe what happened, including where and when it occurred, how you acted, and what the results were. [Probe for details.]
>
> To what extent have you applied your learning from the program in this kind of incident? [Code for the extent to which the person realizes he or she is acting differently as a result of learning from the program: Not at all, somewhat, significantly.]
>
> *For work associate of the participant*
> Think about an incident, or incidents, that happened on the job since [name] has participated in the action learning program. To what extent have you realized he or she is acting differently? In what way? [Probe for details.]

peers, or subordinates of participants. An example of how a critical incident question can be phrased is found in Exhibit 7.2. In phrasing such questions, it is important to have the respondent provide as much detail as possible.

Semistructured or phenomenological interviews with both participants and people who work with participants can be conducted after they complete the program. We have successfully used this method in programs, typically conducting the interviews a few months after the participants have completed the program. A typical interview lasts forty-five minutes to an hour, following a standard set of six or seven questions. The responses to each question are followed up with probes for specific detail.

Interviews should be positioned with interviewees as helping the company learn more about the strengths of the program and opportunities for its improvement, not as evaluations of the participants. This is, in fact, how we view the assessment process. Assessment is a learning opportunity for both the company and those trying to develop this form of learning intervention. We typically record these interviews for detailed coding and analysis. It goes without saying that these interviews should be done by a trained researcher.

The core questions should be tailored to the goals of the program. These interviews typically begin with broad questions to assess overall perception of the experience now that participants have some distance from the experience. The questions should become increasingly focused on specifics, asking about the extent to which the participant realizes he or she is thinking, acting, and reflecting differently on events and the results of these changes in his or her thinking. Equally important are questions on how the organization is operating differently, and with what results. As with any other data-gathering interview, details are important. It is also important for the interviewer to act in such a way that the respondent finds it acceptable to report *no* changes.

Dilworth and Willis (Chapter Five) have successfully asked executives to write essays on their experience. These essays are coded for critical incidents, and qualitative data analysis software has been used to sort the data into categories. The result is a clear pattern of the kind of learning derived from the program.

In terms of quantitative assessment of the learning, if a good 360-degree feedback instrument is used as part of the program, this information can be aggregated and tracked and can provide some additional triangulation. The 360-degree instruments we have used include scales developed for the specific competencies targeted by the program. They also include the opportunity for respondents to write comments.

Despite the success of action learning, there is still much to learn. In conducting assessments, we combine a desire to learn about the impact of the program on the organization and participants with the building of a research agenda. One way we have done this is through the use of a field observer in the program. This person interacts with participants and learning coaches, taking a "helicopter" view of the program as it unfolds. The field notes and opportunistic discussions with participants that this affords enhance the learning from interviews and other data-gathering methods. The field observer also adds value to the program through judicious observations to the learning coaches. In referring to the field observer role, we have used the metaphor of a "sophisticated barbarian" — someone familiar with the learning theory on which the program is based but not directly involved with its development or implementation (Yorks et al., 1996). This approach requires the researcher to make many careful judgments about boundaries, but also provides data not accessible in any other manner.

Conclusion

We leave Susan and her colleagues to make decisions about which school of action learning best fits the needs of their organization and how the program should be designed and implemented. They also need to get management involvement in these decisions. Action learning in an organizational context needs to be part of a coherent strategy of management development and organizational change, not an add-on to a menu of training choices. Too many questions are raised in the minds of participants for action learning to slip comfortably into the organization.

Although we have stressed the relationship among organizational culture, intended learning outcomes, underlying philosophy of action learning, and program design, making choices around action learning is not a mechanistic process. The models we have presented are constructions based on our experience and research. We continue to learn more about the connections among the complex factors that determine learning effectiveness and the rich variations that can be created in practice. There are basic principles on which action learning practice is based. However, the notion of action learning orthodoxy is contrary to the whole enterprise of action learning with its understanding of the importance of Q learning. Accordingly, we offer the frameworks in this book as a starting point for practitioners as they develop their own questioning insight in meeting the unique organizational challenges that confront them.

References

ARL Inquiry. (1997). Using the Burke-Litwin model as a lens for understanding the implications of action reflection learning as a catalyst for organizational change. In R. J. Torraco (Ed.), *Academy of Human Resource Development Conference Proceedings*. Baton Rouge, LA: Academy of Human Resource Development.

Fisher, D., & Torbert, W. R. (1995). *Personal and organizational transformations: The true challenge of continual quality improvement.* New York: McGraw-Hill.

Marquardt, M. J. (1996). *Building the learning organization.* New York: McGraw-Hill.

Marsick, V. J., & Watkins, K. (forthcoming). *Making learning strategic.* Brookfield, VT: Gower.

Senge, P. M. (1990). *The fifth discipline: The art and practice of the learning organization.* New York: Doubleday Currency.

Torbert, W. R. (1991). *The power of balance: Transforming self, society, and scientific inquiry.* Thousand Oaks, CA: Sage.

Watkins, K., & Marsick, V. J. (1993). *Sculpting the learning organization: Lessons in the art and science of systemic change.* San Francisco: Jossey-Bass.

Yorks, L., O'Neil, J., Marsick, V. J., Nilson, G., & Kolodny, R. (1996). Boundary management in action reflection learning research: Taking the role of a sophisticated barbarian. *Human Resource Development Quarterly 7,* 313–329.

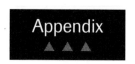

Appendix

▲ Resources for Action Learning

Mary B. Ragno

There are numerous resources available for learning more about action learning. One important source is the International Foundation for Action Learning (IFAL). Information about IFAL can be found on the Internet at: http://www.mentat.co.uk/park/ifal/home.htm.

Membership in IFAL offers a communication link to others who share an interest in action learning. Benefits include a newsletter, a listing of meetings and conferences across the globe, reviews of new books, and access to a considerable lending library of action learning literature.

An excellent source for extending an understanding of action learning is a special issue of the *Performance Improvement Quarterly*, 11(1), 1998. This issue, edited by Lex Dilworth, provides contributions written for a number of perspectives. The foundations of action learning theory, good information on methods and techniques, and examples of application are included.

Scientific School

Pedler, M. (Ed.). (1997). *Action learning in practice.* Hampshire, England, and Brookfield, VT: Gower. This book will familiarize newcomers to action learning with descriptions and some examples of different interpretations of action learning. Part I includes two chapters written by Reginald Revans.

Revans, R. Much of Reg Revans's work is available to IFAL members and others from the IFAL lending library, which is accessible through the Web site (see above). Some of this work, including early discussion papers, is not available elsewhere. Copies of items can often be purchased for the price of photocopies. A full listing of publications available at the library can be requested from Pam Wright, IFAL Administrator, Department of Management Learning, Lancaster University, Lancaster, LA1 4YX; or e-mail: p.wright@lancaster.ac.uk.

Experiential School

Employee Counselling Today, The Journal of Workplace Learning, 8(6). This journal, published in the United Kingdom, is an excellent source of well-written articles about experiences in working with action learning. In particular, the articles by P. Cusins and R. L. Dilworth contain ideas about the use of action learning for practical application in the workplace.

McGill, I., & Beaty, L. (1995). *Action learning: A guide for professional, management and educational development.* London: Kogan Page. This primer for action learning functions as a handy reference for use while working in action learning sets.

Mumford, A. (1995). *Learning at the top.* New York: McGraw-Hill. In Part II, Mumford outlines how managers can use action learning to improve their management skills and performance.

Mumford, A. (Ed.). (1997). *Action learning at work.* Hampshire, England, and Brookfield, VT: Gower. This is a collection of writings from action learning experiences with the International Management Centre's M.B.A. program. Parts II, III, and IV provide examples of experiential action learning.

Pedler, M. (1996). *Action learning for managers.* London: Lemos & Crane. This small, simply written, how-to book of action learning contains material that might be distributed as part of a first-time action learning manager's experience.

Pedler, M. (Ed.). (1997). *Action learning in practice.* Hampshire, England, and Brookfield, VT: Gower. The book provides insights into set advising, tailoring programs to suit different organizational needs, and some thoughts on how to evaluate action learning programs.

Critical Reflection School

Brooks, A., & Watkins, K. E. (Eds.). (1994). *The emerging power of action technologies.* New Directions for Adult and Continuing Education, no. 63. San Francisco: Jossey-Bass. Action learning is presented as one technology for improving inquiry through action and reflection. Articles are forward looking and show that action learning can be applied across many different contexts.

Marquardt, M. J. (1999). *Action learning in action: Transforming problems and people for world-class organizaitonal learning.* Palo Alto, CA: Davies-Black. This book discusses the development and use of critical reflection in action learning programs.

Mezirow, J., (Ed.) (1990). *Fostering critical reflection in adulthood.* San Francisco: Jossey-Bass. This is an informative although complex book that deals with the concepts and dimensions of critical reflection. In particular, see the chapter by V. J. Marsick, "Action Learning and Reflection in the Workplace," pp. 23–46.

West, G. W. (1996). Group learning in the workplace. In S. Imel (Ed.), *Learning in groups: Exploring fundamental principles, new uses, and emerging opportunities.* New Directions for Adult and Continuing Education, no. 71, pp. 51–60. This chapter describes how the process of dialogue can lead beyond adaptive to generative learning in organizations and individuals.

Tacit or Incidental School

Dotlich, D. L., & Noel, J. L. (1998). *Action learning.* San Francisco, CA: Jossey-Bass. This book provides a number of examples of program designs, many of which fit the tacit school.

Downham, T. A., Noel, J. L., & Prendergast, A. E. (1992). Executive development. *Human Resource Management,* 31(1 & 2), pp. 95–107. This article describes two programs that most closely fit the tacit school.

Imel, S. (Ed.). (1996). *Learning in groups: Exploring fundamental principles, new uses, and emerging opportunities.* New Directions for Adult and Continuing Education, no. 71. Group learning plays a significant part in the success of action learning teams. In particular, see P. Cranton's chapter, "Types of Group Learning," pp. 25–32.

Index

A

Academy of Human Resource Development, 1–2

Action learning: adaptability of, 34; definition of, 3; definitions of, by different researchers, 5–6; facilitation of, by learning coach, 39–53; foundation of, 3–4; for personal development, 75–82; resources for evaluations of, 117

Action Learning: A Guide for Professional, Management, and Educational Development (McGill and Beaty), 115

Action learning design: Belgium model for, 22–23; considerations for, 19–20; for critical reflection school, 32; for experiential school, 30–31; needs assessment for, 19; problems and settings in, 20–24; and Revans's model of exchange, 20–21, 23; for scientific school, 29; for tacit school, 33

Action learning implementation: assessment of learning in, 109–111; and choosing an action learning approach, 96–101; decision table for choosing approach for, 98–100; design for, 101–105; familiar versus unfamiliar settings and problems in, 104; individual versus organizational problem in, 104–105; key design characteristics summary for, 102–103; and learning transfer and culture change, 105–107; and links to organizational learning, 107–109; selecting participants for, 105; timing in, 105

Action learning initiative: codesign of, by consultants and organization, 34; implementation considerations for, 34–37; time and space issues in, 27–30

Action learning interventions: and challenging the group, 49–50; and critical reflection, 48–49; enabling role of learning in, 49; invisibility of coach in, 50; methods and practices for, 44–50; outcomes of, 35; and questioning, 48; and reflection, 48–49; and relation to schools of practice, 46–47; and task, 49; and transfer of learning coach skills, 50; as work of learning coach, 44–45

Action learning practice: critical reflection school of, 9–12; experimental school of, 8–9; scientific school of, 6–8; tacit or incidental school of, 12–13

Action learning programs: noise in, 13; pyramid for, 14

Action Learning for Managers (Pedler), 115, 117

Action Learning in Practice (Pedler), 116, 117

Action Learning at Work (Mumford), 115, 117

Action reflection learning program, 5

ARAMARK, 9

Argyris, C., 45, 54, 58, 86, 94

ARL Inquiry, 87, 106, 109, 112

Arnell, E., 12, 18, 25, 28, 36, 37

117

B

Backward-reaching high road transfer, 59
Bailey, C., 19, 37
Baldwin, T. T., 59, 62, 69
Bates, R. A., 69
Bateson, G., 16, 58
Bavetta, A. G., 59
Beaty, L., 4, 8–9, 17, 24–25, 28, 33, 37, 39, 40–42, 48–49, 52, 54, 115
Bennett, R., 43, 54
Beyer, J. M., 84, 85
Bourner, T., 31, 40, 48, 54
Briggs, G. E., 62
Brooks, A., 55, 116
Butterfield, E. C., 56,

C

Carvalho, M. B., 69
Casey, D., 8, 16, 29, 33, 36, 40–42, 48, 50, 54
Cederholm, L., 5, 12, 16, 26, 28, 32–33, 36, 41, 55, 58, 61
Cell, E., 11, 16, 58
Charan, R., 12, 17, 28, 33, 37
Coghill, N., 23, 36
Columbia University, Teachers College, 78
CONOCO Learning Labs, 25–26, 75
Corporate culture. *See* Organizational culture
Critical incidents, 109–111
Critical reflection school: and action learning practice, 9–12; design for, 32; goals of, 10; resources for, 116
Cuozzo, P., 19, 37
Culture, derivation of, 84
Culture change: components of, 86–93; and culture change process, 92–93; and derivation of culture, 85; implications of, 93–94; and learning transfer, 105–107; and model components and effects, 88; implications of, 93–94
Cusins, P., 115

D

Deal, T. E., 84, 95
Deans, J., 57
Dennis, C. B., 16, 26, 28, 32–33, 36, 61
Dilworth, R. L., 19, 23, 25, 37, 78, 101, 104, 111, 114, 115
Diversity, 26–27
Dixon, N., 61
Dotlich, D. L., 117
Double-loop learning, 58
Downham, T. A., 12, 17, 117

E

Ellis, H. C., 62
Emerging Power of Action Teaching, The (Brooks and Watkins), 116
Employee Counseling Today: The Journal of Workplace Learning, 115
Exchange options model (Revans), 20, 21
Experiential learning cycle (Kolb), 8–9
Experiential school: and action learning practice, 8–9; action learning design for, 30–31; resources for, 115–116
Expert solution, 26

F

Far transfer, 56
Federal Deposit Insurance Corporation (FDIC), 75
Field observer, 111
Fine, G., 84, 95
Fisher, D., 106, 112
Ford, J. K., 69
Forward-reaching high road transfer, 59
Fosbury flop, 10

Fostering Critical Reflection in Adulthood (Mezirow), 116
Foy, N., 8, 17, 19, 37

G
Garatt, B., 48, 49, 54
General Electric (GE), 75
General Electric Company (GEC), 8, 13
Gibson, A., 48, 54
Gielen, E.W.M., 59
Gist, M. E., 59, 62
Globalization, 106
Goldstein, I. L., 69
"Group Learning in the Workplace" (West), 116
Group projects: basic framing criteria for, 24; and forming groups, 26–27; and ideal group size, 26; versus individual projects, 24–26

H
Harries, J. M., 40–41, 54
Harrison, R., 48, 54
Harvard University, 29
Havighurst, R. J., 61
Heinzmann, A. T., 62
Holton, III, E. F., 69, 70
Honey-Mumford Learning Style Questionnaire, 45, 77
Hospital Internal Communication (HIC) Study, 23

I
Imel, S., 116
Incidental learning, 12. *See also* Tacit school
Individual projects, versus group projects, 25–26
Inglis, S., 36, 37, 40, 43, 48, 54
International Foundation of Action Learning (IFAL), 1–2, 114–115

J
Jones, H., 56–57
Just-in-time learning, 33

K
Kazanas, H. J., 19, 38
Kennedy, A. A., 84, 95
Kolb, D., 8–9, 17, 45, 54
Kolodny, R., 18, 20, 37, 38, 55, 111, 113
Komaki, J., 62
Kontoghiorghes, C., 58

L
Laker, D. R., 56
Lamm, S., 12, 17, 56–57
Lancaster University, 115
Lawlor, A., 40, 54
Lawrence, J., 40, 42–43, 49, 54
Lawson, L., 62
Learning: assessment of, 109–111; Preston definition of, 8; Revans definition of, 7; and situation learning, Cell definition of, 7, 58
Learning coaches: background of, 41; characteristics of, 42–43; in experiential school, 9; and external coaches, 52; and group process skills, 42–43; and internal coaches, 51–52; and learning interventions, 44–45; necessity for, 40–41; personal competencies of, 44; role of, 39–53; in scientific school, 3, 8; and systems thinking, 43; training of, 52–53
Learning content, validity of, 70
Learning in Groups: Exploring Fundamental Principles, New Uses, and Emerging Opportunities (Imel), 116

Learning interventions: and challenging the group, 49–50; and critical reflection, 48–49; and enabling learning, 49; and invisibility of coach, 50; methods and practices for, 44–50; and questioning, 48; and reflection, 48–49; relation of, to schools of practice, 46–47; and task, 49; and transfer of learning coach skills, 50

Learning at the Top (Mumford), 115

Learning transfer: around competencies, 87; and culture change, 105–109; objective to help bring about, 68; and patterns of design observed from the field, 64–65; and transfer climate, 69–77; and transfer design practices in corporate programs, 65–66

Learning transfer climate questionnaire (LTQ), 69

Lemback, M., 69

Lessem, R., 8–9, 17

Level III learning (Bateson), 58

Level II learning (Bateson), 7

Lotz, S., 41, 55

Low road transfer, 59

M

Marquardt, M. J., 107, 112, 116

Marsick, V. J., 1, 4, 10, 12, 16, 17, 18, 20, 24, 35, 37, 38, 39, 40–42, 48–51, 54, 55, 58, 96, 107–109, 111–113

Massachusetts Institute of Technology, 29

Mathieu, J. E., 69

McGehee, W., 61

McGill, I., 4, 8–9, 17, 24, 25, 28, 33, 37, 39, 40–42, 48–49, 52, 54, 115

McLaughlin, R., 8–9, 17

McNamara, M., 6, 17, 28, 37

McNulty, N. G., 4, 17, 29

Meaning schemes, 7, 58, 61

Mezirow, J., 10, 17, 58, 78, 116

Miller, S., 48, 54

Mumford, A., 5, 8–9, 17, 25–26, 37, 40, 45, 54, 115, 117

N

National Semiconductor, 75

Naylor, J. C., 62

Nelson, G. D., 56

Nilson, G. E., 18, 20, 37, 38, 55, 83, 105, 107, 111, 113

Noel, J. L., 12, 17, 28, 33, 37, 117

Noise, definition of, 13–14

O

O'Neil, J., 1, 6, 9–10, 12, 15, 18, 19–20, 24, 26, 28, 35–36, 37, 38, 39–42, 48, 55, 56, 96, 101, 104, 111, 113

O'Neil, J. A., 37, 40, 42–45, 48–50, 53, 55

Organizational change: and assessment of learning, 109–111; and critical incident question samples, 110; and culture change, 105–107

Organizational culture: and components of cultural change, 86–93; and culture change model components and effects, 88; and culture change process, 92–93; definition of, 83–86; and exhibiting cultural components, 87–90, and implications of cultural change, 93–94; reinforcing and refining cultural components in, 92; and sanctioning cultural components, 91–92; and symbolizing cultural components, 90–91

Organizational learning, links to, 107–109

P

P learning, 15, 23, 31–33, 61, 70
Pearce, D., 8, 16, 29, 33, 36, 42, 55
Pedler, M., 4, 10, 18, 33, 37, 40–41, 43–44, 55, 114, 115–116
Performance goals, 62–63
Performance Improvement Quarterly, 25, 114
Perkins, D. N., 59
Personal development, 75–82
Perspective transformation, 58
Prendergast, A. E., 12, 17, 117
Preston, P., 8, 18
Procter & Gamble, 75
Program design practices, 63–64
Programmed instruction, 7
Programmed learning (P learning), 31–33
Putnam, R., 45, 54

Q

Q learning (Revans), 58, 61
Questioning insight, 3, 7

R

Ragno, M. B., 114
Reber, R. A., 59, 62
Reddy, W. B., 42, 55
Reflection: in critical reflection school, 10; in experiential school, 9
Reflection and dialogue technique (R&D), 90–91
Revans, R. W., 3–4, 6–7, 15, 18, 20–24, 26, 37, 38, 39–40, 44, 55, 58, 61, 75, 78, 114–115
Rothwell, W. J., 19, 38
Rouiller, J. Z., 69
Royer, J. M., 56
Ruona, W.E.A., 69

S

Salas, E., 69
Salomon, G., 59
Schein, E. H., 42, 55, 84, 95
Schön, D. A., 52, 55, 58, 86, 94
Scientific school: and action learning practice, 6–8; design for, 29; resources for, 114–115
Senge, P. M., 10, 18, 107, 113
Sewerin, T., 42, 44, 55
Seyler, D. L., 69
Situation learning, Cell's definition of, 7, 58
Smith, D. M., 45, 54
Stevens, C. K., 59
Stewart, J., 23, 36
Systems thinking, 43

T

Tacit school: and action learning practice, 12–13; design for, 33; resources for, 116
Tannenbaum, S. I., 69
Thayer, P. W., 61
Theories in practice (Argyris and Schön), 86
Thorpe, R., 8–9, 17
Torbert, W. R., 106, 112, 113
Training transfer: four factors in, 69–71; some basic concepts of, 61
Transfer of learning: conceptualization of, 57–60; and implications for design, 63–64; to organizational setting, 56–72; program design from perspective of, 60–64. *See also* Learning transfer
Transformative learning, 76, 78–81
Transsituational learning, 11, 58
Trice, H. M., 84, 85
TRW, 13, 75

Tuckman, B. W., 45, 55
Turner, E., 5, 12, 18, 25, 28, 37, 55

U

Unisys, 75

V

Vicere, A. A., 9, 18
Volvo Truck, 25

W

Wallin, J. A., 59, 62
Watkins, K. E., 10, 12, 16, 24, 37, 40–41, 54, 55, 107–109, 112–113, 116
Weeks, W. H., 6, 17
Weinstein, K., 2, 10, 11, 18, 24, 26, 28, 31, 33, 38, 40, 42, 48–52, 54, 55
West, F. W., 116
Wexley, K. N., 59, 62
Whirlpool, 75
Willis, V. J., 56–57, 78, 104, 111
Wright, P., 115

Y

Yorks, L., 1, 12, 16, 20, 26, 28, 32, 33, 36, 37, 38, 50, 55, 56–57, 61, 64, 96, 111, 113
Yukl, G., 69

▲ The Authors

Robert L. Dilworth is an assistant professor at Virginia Commonwealth University, where he coordinates the human resource development program. He has a broad range of experience with action learning and is a colleague of Reginald W. Revans, the principal pioneer of action learning. In 1998 Dilworth edited two special issues of the *Performance Improvement Quarterly* on action learning.

Sharon Lamm is president of Lamm Associates, Ltd., and a doctoral candidate at Teachers College, Columbia University. She is experienced in implementing a wide range of management development programs and serves as an action learning coach.

Victoria J. Marsick is a professor in the Department of Organization and Leadership at Teachers College, Columbia University. She consults with both private and public organizations and is in wide demand as a speaker on learning organizations. Marsick's many books include *Sculpting the Learning Organization* and *Incidental Learning in the Workplace* (both coauthored with Karen Watkins). She has served on the Board of the Academy of Human Resource Development and is a past chair of the Research Committee of the American Society for Training and Development.

Glenn E. Nilson is a principal of Glenn Associates. Until recently he served as chair of the Department of Sociology at Eastern Connecticut

State University. His expertise is in group and team development, action learning, learning communities, and organizational learning, and he has worked with a wide range of organizations in these areas. He has participated in a research consortium of faculty and consultants on organizational learning and with other members of the consortium has published numerous articles on action learning.

Judy O'Neil, of Partners for the Learning Organization, has wide experience in the design and implementation of action learning programs and has published widely on the topic. She is president of the U.S. chapter of the International Federation for Action Learning and serves as adjunct faculty at Teachers College, Columbia University, and Eastern Connecticut State University.

Mary B. Ragno is a consultant to child nutrition programs, Connecticut State Department of Education. She is an action learning coach and a teaching assistant to action learning classes. She is presently a doctoral candidate in adult education at Teachers College, Columbia University.

Verna J. Willis is an associate professor at Georgia State University, where she established the human resource development program. In 1997 this program was named "most outstanding" by the Academy of Human Resource Development. Willis has extensive action learning background and experience and has done work with the Revans Centre for Action Learning and Research at the University of Salford in England. In 1998 she was involved with action learning research in England, Romania, and the Ivory Coast of Africa.

Lyle Yorks is professor of management and chair of the Department of Business Administration at Eastern Connecticut State University, where he established and coordinates the master of science in organizational management program. The author or coauthor of nine books, he has published in a wide range of professional journals including *Academy of Management Review, California Management Review, Human Resource Development Quarterly,* and *Sloan Management Review.* He has broad experience in both researching and implementing action learning programs.

Academy of Human Resource Development

The Academy of Human Resource Development (AHRD) is a global organization made up of, governed by, and created for the human resource development (HRD) scholarly community of academics and reflective practitioners. The Academy was formed to encourage systematic study of human resource development theories, processes, and practices; to disseminate information about HRD; to encourage the application of HRD research findings; and to provide opportunities for social interaction among individuals with scholarly and professional interests in HRD from multiple disciplines and from across the globe.

AHRD membership includes a subscription to *Advances in Developing Human Resources, Human Resource Development Quarterly,* and *Human Resource Development International.* A partial list of other benefits includes (1) membership in the only global organization dedicated to advancing the HRD profession through research, (2) annual research conference with full proceedings of research papers (900 pages), (3) reduced prices on professional books, (4) subscription to the *Forum,* the academy newsletter, and (5) research partnering, funding, and publishing opportunities. Senior practitioners are encouraged to join AHRD's Global 100!

Academy of Human Resource Development
P.O. Box 25113
Baton Rouge, LA 70894-511
USA

Phone: 225-334-1874
Fax: 225-334-1875
E-mail: office@ahrd.org
Website: http://www.ahrd.org

"At last! Practical approaches for moving past tired old training content toward more meaningful, measurable results. *Running Training Like a Business* is a must-read."

—Steve Roerich, Vice President, Worldwide Quality and Business Improvement, Johnson & Johnson

Hardcover, 200 pages,
6-1/8 x 9-1/4
Available May 1999
ISBN 1-57675-059-0
Item no. 50590-602
U.S. $27.95 (CAN $40.95)

Berrett-Koehler
San Francisco

Running Training Like a Business

Delivering Unmistakable Value

David van Adelsberg & Edward A. Trolley

- Addresses training's central challenge—how to meet organizational demands for clear business value
- Provides fresh and powerful strategic perspectives and tools to take training out of the limbo between "doing good" and delivering unmistakable value to the business, through a strategic assessment of training operations
- Draws on the authors' great successes running training like a business at major international corporations, including Du Pont, Moore Corporation, and NatWest
- Sets out the steps training organizations must take to transform themselves into operating like a business

Many of today's business leaders champion learning as essential to business success, backing their belief with massive investments in training and development (T&D). At issue, the authors contend, is T&D's inability to seize this opportunity and deliver unmistakable value to its most influential customers: the executives who pay for training services but are unable to see clear business value being returned on their companies' training investments.

Van Adelsberg and Trolley suggest that the key to delivering unmistakable business value lies in transforming T&D in spirit and in practice from a function to a business. The authors draw on their experiences working inside Moore Corporation, Du Pont, Mellon Bank, Kaiser Permanente, Texas Instruments, and other top businesses to illustrate *Running Like a Business*.

- Eliminates the many hidden costs of training
- Refocuses T&D from delivering training content to addressing business issues
- Makes T&D a full strategic partner in business decision making
- Ensures that training measurement is "baked in, not bolted on"
- Improves the effectiveness and efficiency of internal and external T&D organizations

Van Adelsberg and Trolley lead the reader through a proven four-step process for transforming traditional training organizations into training enterprises capable of delivering unmistakable value, quarter after quarter, year after year.

To order call toll-free: **(800) 929-2929**
Internet: www.bkpub.com   Fax: 802-864-7627   Or mail to Berrett-Koehler Publishers, P.O. Box 565, Williston VT 05495

Results

How to Assess Performance, Learning, and Perceptions in Organizations

Richard A. Swanson and Elwood F. Holton III

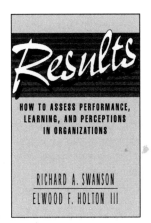

- Shows human resource development (HRD) professionals how to measure organizational results within the domains of performance, learning, and perceptions
- The widely praised Results Assessment System simplifies the complex issues of assessment, enabling HRD professionals to clearly demonstrate their results
- From the author of *Analysis for Improving Performance*, winner of the Outstanding Instructional Communication Award from the International Society for Performance Improvement and the Society for Human Resource Management Book Award

Results presents a practical guide to building a successful, competitive, and cost-effective HRD practice that meets customers' needs. It teaches a highly effective, easy-to-learn, field-tested system for assessing organization results within three domains: performance (system and financial), learning (knowledge and expertise), and perceptions (participant and stakeholder).

Why measure results in HRD? Because the "corporate school" and "human relations" models of HRD practice, whereby development occurs simply because it is good for employees, no longer works. If HRD is to be a core organizational process, it must hold itself accountable. Measuring results, particularly bottom-line performance, is key to gaining support from top management. And those who measure results ultimately find it a source of program improvement and innovation as well as pride and satisfaction.

Results is both theoretically sound and firmly rooted in practice, offering a core five-step assessment process that gives readers a simple and direct journey from analysis inputs to decision outputs. Whether they have assessment tools but no theory, theory but no tools, or no tools and no theory, this book will equip them to quickly and effectively assess their results.

"*Results* presents the most practical and proven assessment system for the profession"—
Kent Dubbe,
Vice President
of Human Resources,
Longaberger Company

Hardcover, approx.
280 pages
Available April 1999
ISBN 1-57675-004-2 CIP
Item no. 50442-266-602
$34.95

Berrett-Koehler
San Francisco

To order call toll-free: **(800) 929-2929**
Internet: www.bkpub.com   Fax: 802-864-7627   Or mail to
Berrett-Koehler Publishers, P.O. Box 565, Williston VT 05495

Books from Berrett-Koehler Publishers

Human Resource Development Research Handbook
Linking Research and Practice
Richard A. Swanson and Elwood F. Holton III, Editors

THE *Human Resource Development Research Handbook* gives practitioners the tools they need to stay on the leading edge of the profession. Each chapter is written in straightforward language by a leading researcher and offers real-world examples to clearly show how research and theory are not just for academics, but are practical tools to solve everyday problems.

Paperback, 225 pages, 3/97 • ISBN 1-881052-68-0 CIP • Item no. 52680-602 $24.95

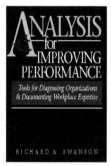

Analysis for Improving Performance
Tools for Diagnosing Organizations and Documenting Workplace Expertise
Richard A. Swanson

ANALYSIS FOR Improving Performance details the front-end work essential to the success of any performance improvement effort. In clear language and easy-to-follow steps, Swanson shows how to do the rigorous preparatory analysis that defines and shapes successful performance improvement efforts, and maps the critical steps for ensuring that a performance improvement program will meet real business needs and objectives.

Paperback, 298 pages, 9/96 • ISBN 1-57675-001-9 CIP • Item no. 50019-602 $24.95
Hardcover, 7/94 • ISBN 1-881052-48-6 CIP • Item no. 52486 $34.95

Structured On-the-Job Training
Unleashing Employee Expertise in the Workplace
Ronald Jacobs and Michael Jones

JACOB AND JONES describe an approach to on-the-job training that combines the structure of off-site training with the inherent efficiency of training conducted in the actual job setting. They show how structured OJT helps employees bridge the gap between learning job information and actually using that information on the job. *Structured On-the-Job Training* provides step-by-step guidelines for designing and delivering effective training in the actual job setting.

Hardcover, 220 pages, 1/95 • ISBN 1-881052-20-6 CIP • Item no. 52206-602 $29.95

Available at your favorite bookstore, or call (800) 929-2929

CALL FOR PAPERS
Academy of Human Resource Development
2000 ANNUAL CONFERENCE

Sheraton Imperial Hotel • Raleigh-Durham, NC • March 7–12, 2000
P.O. Box 25113, Baton Rouge, LA 70894 USA, 504-334-1874,
Fax 504-334-1875

The Academy of HRD, an international organization with the mission of encouraging the systematic study of human resource development theories, processes, and practices, encourages you to submit proposals for the 2000 Annual Conference.

All scholars interested in HRD are invited to submit proposals for consideration. The conference is attended by researchers and graduate students in HRD, business, psychology, education, economics, sociology, technology, and communication. In addition, HRD researchers and reflective practitioners from business, industry, and governments participate fully in the conference.

Proposals will be blind reviewed and should consist of new, unpublished research. Papers accepted for the conference program will be published in the conference proceedings and may be published elsewhere following the conference.

Submission Requirements
Authors may submit full manuscripts or proposals. Full manuscripts are strongly encouraged, but abbreviated proposals of 4–5 pages will also be accepted. Manuscripts presenting data-based studies should minimally contain the following elements:

1. Title
2. Problem statement and theoretical framework
3. Research questions and/or hypotheses
4. Methodology
5. Results, conclusions, and limitations
6. Discussion of how this research contributes to new knowledge in HRD

AHRD also welcomes manuscripts presenting new scholarly theory, models, conceptual analyses, literature reviews, and case studies. These papers must also follow the above outline as closely as possible.

Submission Deadlines

Proposals/manuscripts: *October 1, 1999*
Decision notification: *November 16, 1999*
Final papers due to proceedings editor: *January 5, 2000*

Manuscript Requirements

Proposals/manuscripts should meet the following criteria:

1. Typed, double spaced.
2. Should not exceed 20 pages including figures and references (final papers limited to 8 single-spaced pages). Manuscripts that exceed 20 pages will be returned.
3. Blind review ready.
   A. Cover sheet with author(s) identification.
   B. No author identification in body, header, or footer of manuscript.
4. Cover sheet should contain full identification and contact information for *all* authors.
5. All communication with authors will be via e-mail so proposal/manuscript submissions ***must include an e-mail address for all authors***.
6. All deadlines are *firm*. Exceptions will be made only for true emergencies or extraordinary circumstances.
7. All final manuscripts must include a disk copy in MS Word 6.0 (or later) format.

Submission Addresses

Submission by e-mail attachment is strongly preferred. Do not send duplicate manuscripts. If an e-mail submission does not go through, you will be given time to submit a faxed or mailed copy of the manuscript.

E-mail Address
office @ahrd.org

Manuscripts sent as e-mail attachments should specify the word processing format.

Mailing Address
Academy of Human Resource Development
Attn: Conference Chair
P.O. Box 25113
Baton Rouge, LA 70894-5113

Address for Overnight Services
Academy of Human Resource Development
Attn: Conference Chair
Louisiana State University
1142 Old Forestry Building
Baton Route, LA 70803